BISCORNU PINCUSHIONS

HOW MANY DO YOU NEED?

ISBN - 978-0-473-77867-5

www.cherryparker.co.nz

CONTENTS

Definition of a Biscornu Pincushion

A biscornu pincushion is a small, puffy, eight -sided, octagonal cushion made from two fabric squares sewn together in a unique offset way and usually indented with a button in the centre.

The word biscornu comes from the French word meaning quirky.

Biscornu pincushions are very popular and come in many sizes. Usually they are embroidered or cross stitched, but the base can be fabric or felt, so only the top is decorated. So many choices!

How Many Biscornu Pincushions do you need?

The answer is - lots!

We most likely need one or two pincushions that we use all the time. I use one for cross stitch needles of every description and another for pins and odd shaped needles that I don't use on a regular basis.

We begin by being fascinated by the shape of a Biscornu pincushion, believing it is too difficult to stitch. People with great embroidery skills are the ones who stitch these interesting pincushions - Wrong!

They are simply two squares of fabric both the same size.

Around the border on the top, are the same number of stitches as around the border on the base. Sewing it together matching stitch for stitch is an easy exercise and the Biscornu is quickly completed. Any pattern can be used on the top or bottom and the method of sewing it together is always the same.

This book includes designs for cats, cherries, owls, roses, patchwork, poppies, houses, coffee, Christmas and Halloween. Three patterns - Patchwork squares, Waste Not, Want Not and the mini biscornus hardly require any pattern at all. Also included is a 15 sided biscornu using more thread from stash and an octopus or two are lurking just for fun.

The problem is not in the sewing, but the temptation to collect and stitch yet another Biscornu design that we love, and so on it goes. It becomes a very addictive hobby. But satisfying and harmless.

ABOUT ME

In 2025 I set myself a personal challenge to stitch a small New Zealand design each day, all of which would fit into a 14" hoop. I put the designs on my Facebook page so that if others were interested they could stitch along as well. Over the year many joined in and others wanted a pattern to stitch for another year. 365 designs were too big for a pattern but a book - yes.

While I was stitching the challenge, I used the odd pieces of thread that I couldn't be bothered winding back on the bobbin, stitching them into a biscornu pincushion. Wondering how many I had designed over the years I added them up on my ETSY page - and you guessed it.
I had enough to put into a book.

But of course I had to add another 5 or 6 for good measure. There always needs to be new patterns in the mix. What a great excuse to stitch a few more - especially my lazy biscornus that don't really need a pattern!

As one of New Zealand's leading cross stitch designers, I have spent decades creating patterns that have been enjoyed worldwide.
My designs have been published in Just CrossStitch magazine in the United States, in Great Britain, also in Australia and many series have run over several years here in New Zealand.
Every one of my designs is personally drawn, stitched and tested before it becomes a pattern for you to enjoy.
This traditional approach takes me longer, but it means every pattern has been tested in the real world.

My problem has always been that while I am stitching the current pattern, my brain has already begun thinking about the next project. Who can resist a new hand dyed fabric or a fancy thread that you have to buy - just in case.

I hope you enjoy these Biscornu patterns as we all need more than we think.

Cherry

READING THE GRAPH

Each square represents one cross stitch.

Each triangle represents one ¾ stitch.

Each symbol represents a different coloured thread.

The darker lines are backstitching lines which add definition.

The background is not stitched.

The designs throughout this book are stitched on 25 count evenweave fabric over two strands of fabric using two strands of thread unless otherwise stated. 14 count Aida can also be used, which will make the design only very fractionally smaller.
DMC threads are used throughout unless otherwise stated.

The back stitching is worked using one strand of thread when all other stitching has been completed.

Pattern layout

Finished design photographs appear on the right-hand page.
Pattern details are shown on the facing pages, with additional
notes continuing onto the following page where required.

THE SIMPLE CROSS STITCH

A cross stitch is a combination of two diagonal stitches of equal length. It is an easy stitch to learn and highly addictive. Whether you work each cross stitch individually, or work a row of diagonal half stitches (1-2) and then stitch back along the row (3-4) to complete the cross stitch is entirely up to you.

I prefer to work each stitch individually as unpicking is easier. Cross stitch can be worked horizontally, vertically or diagonally - whichever you are the most happiest with.
Only one rule applies. Make sure all the stitches are crossed uniformly; that is all the lower stitches lie from left to right (1-2) and all the upper stitches lie from right to left (3-4).

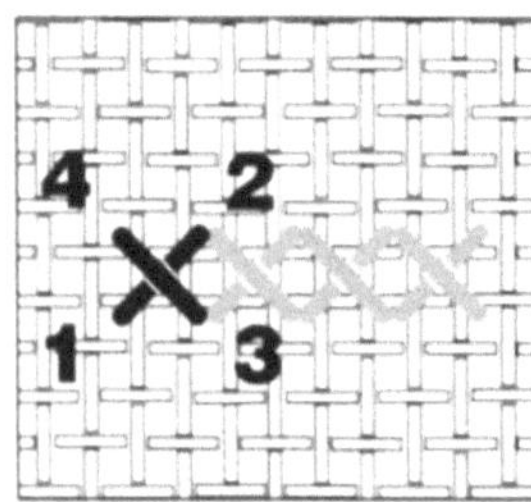

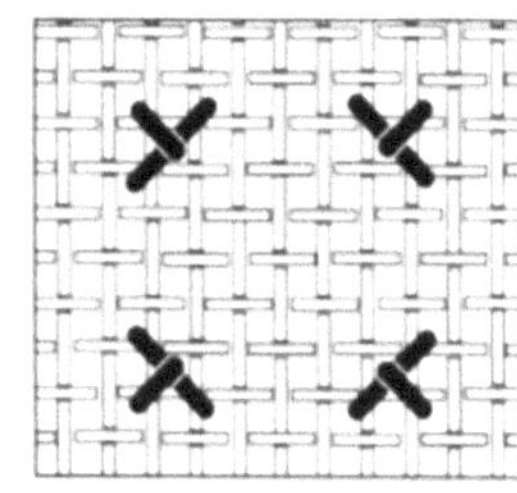
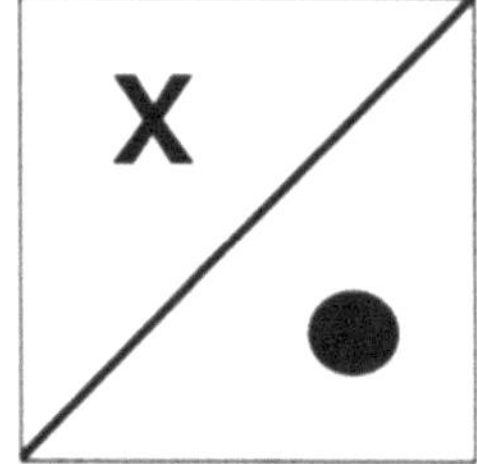

THREE QUARTER STITCH

Always work the longer diagonal stitch of the three-quarter stitch first and then the shorter, top part of the stitch. The three-quarter stitch can be worked on four different angle - see diagrams.
The great advantage of the three-quarter stitch is that it not only gives your work a more natural line, but the stitches are neatly edged and often don't need to be backstitched.

If the square looks like the square at the top right, work two three-quarter stitches in the same square, each with a corresponding colour. This will not be too bulky and the stitches sit neatly when completed. The diagonal line between the two threequarter stitches may not need to be backstitched.

BACKSTITCH

Backstitch is used for outlining, emphasising the design or for lettering and is shown on the graph by a solid black line. It is done after all the cross stitch and three-quarter stitches have been completed, and is usually worked with one strand of thread. To backstitch bring the needle up through the fabric beside the finished stitch at the bottom of the cross stitch, down at the top of the stitch, back out at the bottom of the stitch below and so on.

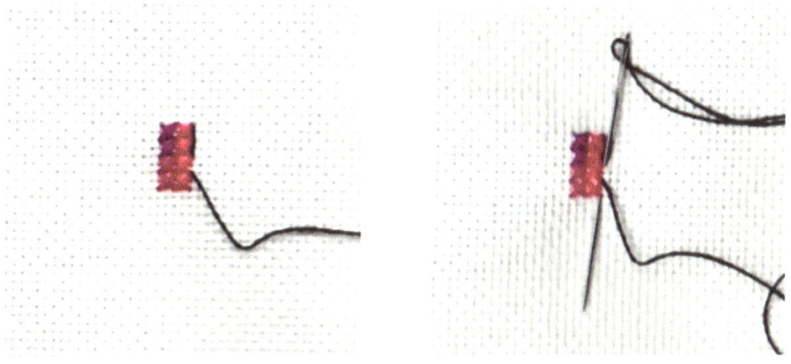

DIFFERENT BUT ALL THE SAME

Every Biscornu is completed in the same way. Many different designs can be used to decorate the top and bottom or as I choose to do - only stitch the top. (With a couple of exceptions).

The base of the pincushion doesn't have to be cross stitched or even cross stitch fabric.
I like to use fabric such as denim, felt and patchwork fabric. As long as both top and bottom squares are exactly the same size, every biscornu comes together in the same way.

The first three patterns give instructions for a -

A - a biscornu with a cross stitched base
B - a biscornu with a fabric base
C - a biscornu with a felt base.

Each design is graphed seperately throughout the book and all completed as above (A,B or C)

The only thing that changes throughout the book is the design on the top, the threads and the size of each biscornu.

There is no hard and fast rule that you have to use the same coloured material or threads that I have used. Look at your own stash and have fun with the colours.

I love to stitch on 25 count evenweave Lugana which stitches up only ever so slightly bigger than 14 count Aida. Just remember if you use a different thread count of fabric this will change the size of your pincushion.

I have used DMC threads throughout as well as hand dyed threads that are clearly defined.

I hope you find a biscornu in the book that you just have to add to your collection.

BEGINNER'S BISCORNU
with cross stitched base.

BEGINNER'S BISCORNU
with cross stitched base.

Design Size:	4" (10cms) square
Stitch Count:	55sts square
Fabric:	25 count Antique White Lugana for the top square 25 count Red Lugana for the base Batting or felt which is optional One button Stuffing of your choice
Threads:	'Farmer's Market' hand dyed threads by Cottage Garden or any other hand dyed or variegated thread.

The design is cross stitched with two strands of thread over two strands of 25 count Lugana fabric. Backstitch the outer line with two strands of thread.

NB - when working with variegated or hand dyed threads, complete each cross stitch as you go, to maintain continuity of colour.

BEGINNER'S BISCORNU
with cross stitched base.

Graph for the top of the pincusion

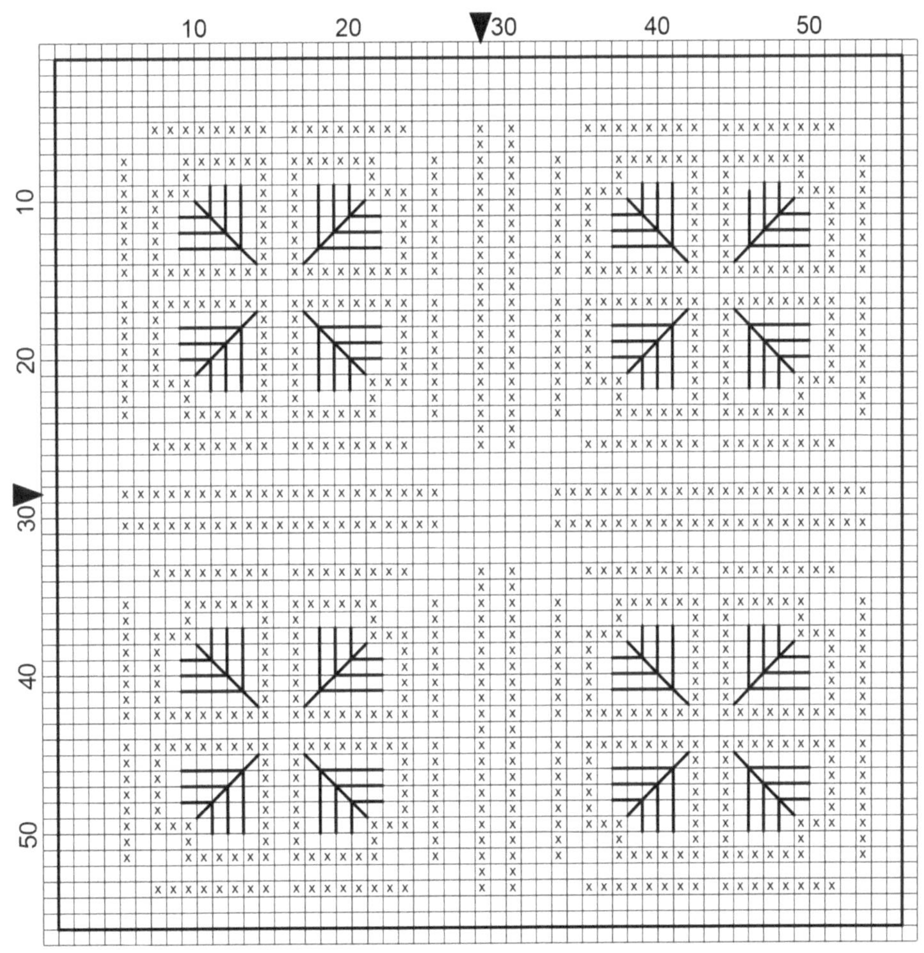

BEGINNER'S BISCORNU
with cross stitched base.

Graph for the base of the pincushion

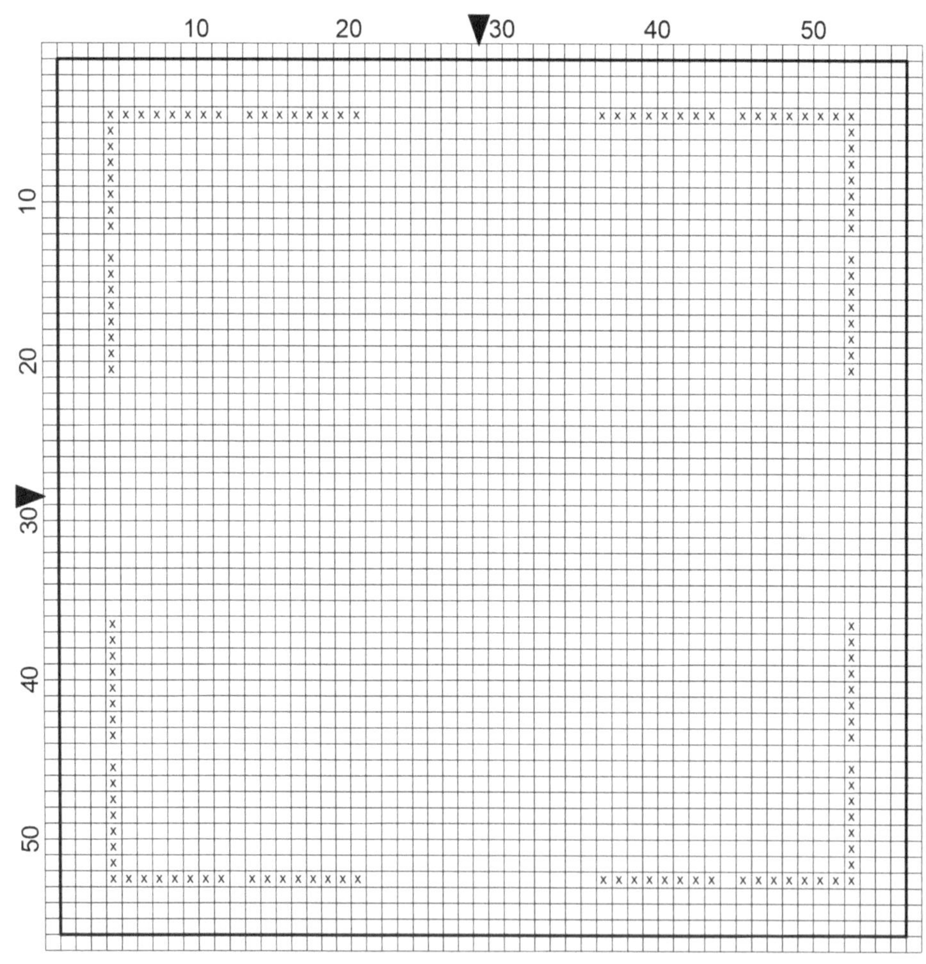

BEGINNER'S BISCORNU
with cross stitched base.

Construction - The outer line on the graph is the **fold line** for the top and the bottom of the pincushion. Backstitch this line with two strands of thread. When all the cross stitching is complete, fold the fabric to the wrong side and tack down with large stitches. To give the top of the pincushion a smooth finish, a piece of batting or felt can be placed on the wrong side of the cross stitch before folding over. This step is optional.

Mark the midpoint of each side of each square with a pin. Using two strands of embroidery thread and with wrong sides facing, whip stitch the base to the top and turning at each 'corner'. Begin at any pin at a halfway point on one side.

Continue whip stitching, stitch for stitch, from base to top, matching corners to centres.

Stitch until seven sides have been joined. Stuff the pincushion and sew the opening closed.

Thread a long needle with a doubled length of strong thread. Bring the needle up from the bottom, through one hole in the button, back down through another hole and return to the bottom of the pincushion. Pull the threads firmly indenting the centre of the pincushion. Cut the threads.

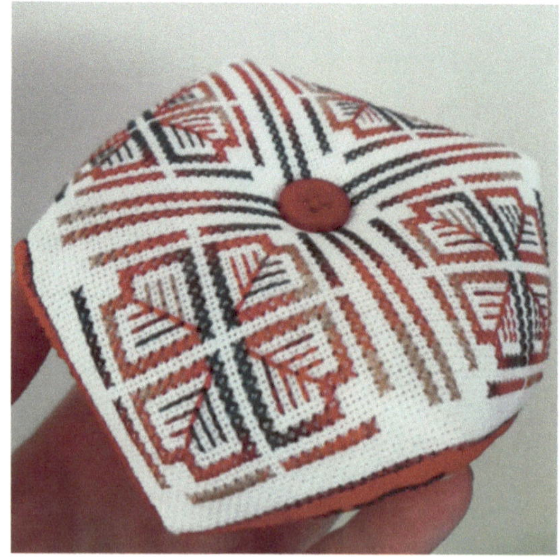

BEGINNER'S BISCORNU
with denim fabric base.

BEGINNER'S BISCORNU
with denim fabric base.

Design Size: 4" (10cms) square

Stitch Count: 51sts square

Fabric: 25 count Antique White Lugana for the top square
Denim fabric cut from an old pair of jeans
Batting or felt which is optional
One button
Stuffing of your choice

Threads: (x) 'Muscat' hand dyed threads by Cottage Garden
or any other hand dyed or variegated thread.
A pale coloured thread of your choice to compliment the hand
dyed thread. I used DMC 931 (O) to add another shade of denim.

The design for the top of the pincushion is cross stitched with two strands of thread over two strands of 25 count Lugana fabric. Backstitch the outer line with two strands of thread to match the denim fabric.

NB - when working with variegated or hand dyed threads complete each cross stitch as you go, to maintain continuity of colour.

BEGINNER'S BISCORNU
with denim fabric base.

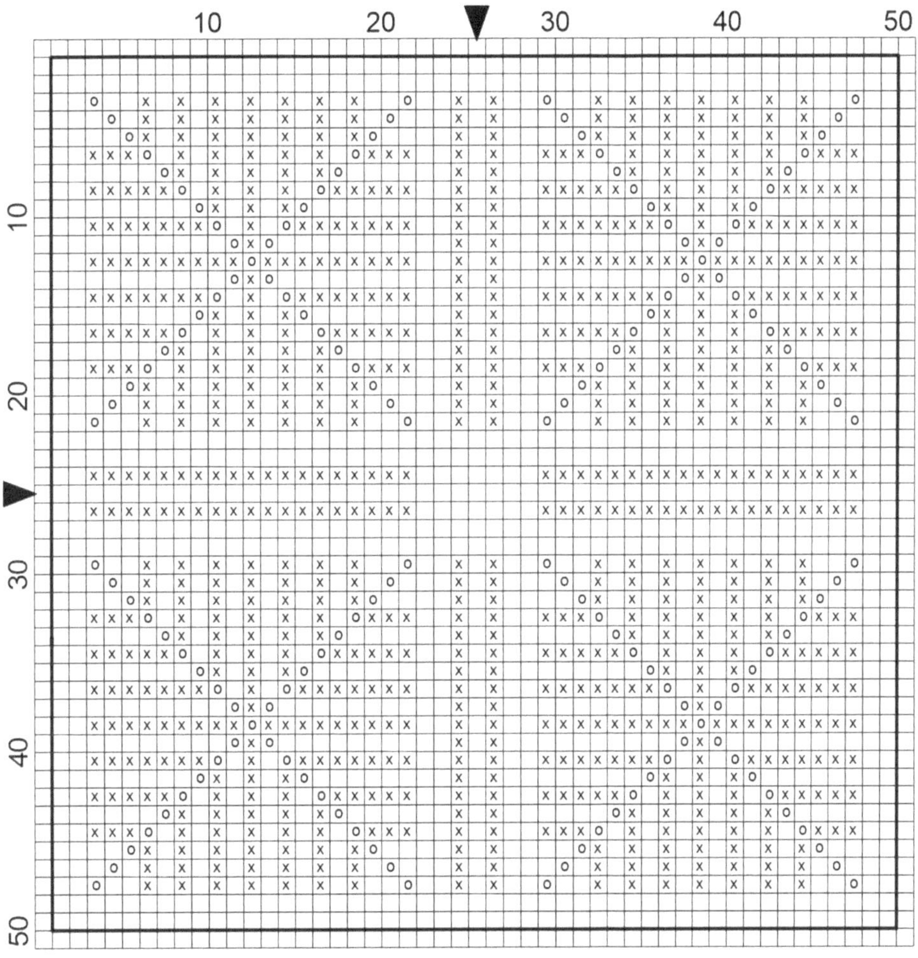

BEGINNER'S BISCORNU
with denim fabric base.

Construction - The outer line on the graph is the **fold line** for the top of the pincushion. Backstitch this line with two strands of thread. When all the cross stitching is complete, fold the fabric, along this line, to the wrong side and tack down with large stitches.

To give the top of the pincushion a smooth finish, a piece of batting or felt can be placed on the wrong side of the cross stitch before folding over. This step is optional.

Cut a square of denim fabric to the same size as the top - **ie with hems included.**

Hem the square of denim as you did with the cross stitch fabric so that both squares of fabric are now exactly the same size.
Mark the midpoint of each square with a pin.

BEGINNER'S BISCORNU
with denim fabric base.

Using two strands of embroidery thread to match the denim fabric and with wrong sides facing, whip stitch the base to the top, turning at each 'corner'. Begin at any pin at a halfway point on one side.

Continue matching corners to centres until seven sides have been joined. Stuff the pincushion and sew the opening closed, pushing the last little bit of stuffing in at the last moment. The biscornu needs to be firm.

BEGINNER'S BISCORNU
with denim fabric base.

Thread a long needle with a doubled length of strong thread. Bring the needle up from the bottom, through one hole in the button, back through another hole and return to the bottom of the pincushion. Pull the threads firmly, indenting the centre of the pincushion.
Secure and cut the threads.

Changing the colour of the threads for the top and using a complementary coloured fabric for the base makes it look like completely different biscornu.

This why we need so many as the options are endless.

BEGINNER'S BISCORNU
with felt base.

BEGINNER'S BISCORNU
with felt base.

Design Size: 4" (10cms) square

Stitch Count: 55sts square

Fabric: 25 count Antique White Lugana for the top square
Grey felt for the base for the base
Batting or felt which is optional
Stuffing of your choice
Button

Threads: 'Albert' hand dyed threads by Cottage Garden
or any other hand dyed variegated thread.

The design for the top of the pincushion is cross stitched with two strands of thread over two strands of 25 count Lugana fabric. Backstitch the outer line with two strands of thread.

NB - when working with variegated or hand dyed threads complete each cross stitch as you go, to maintain continuity of colour.

BEGINNER'S BISCORNU
with felt base.

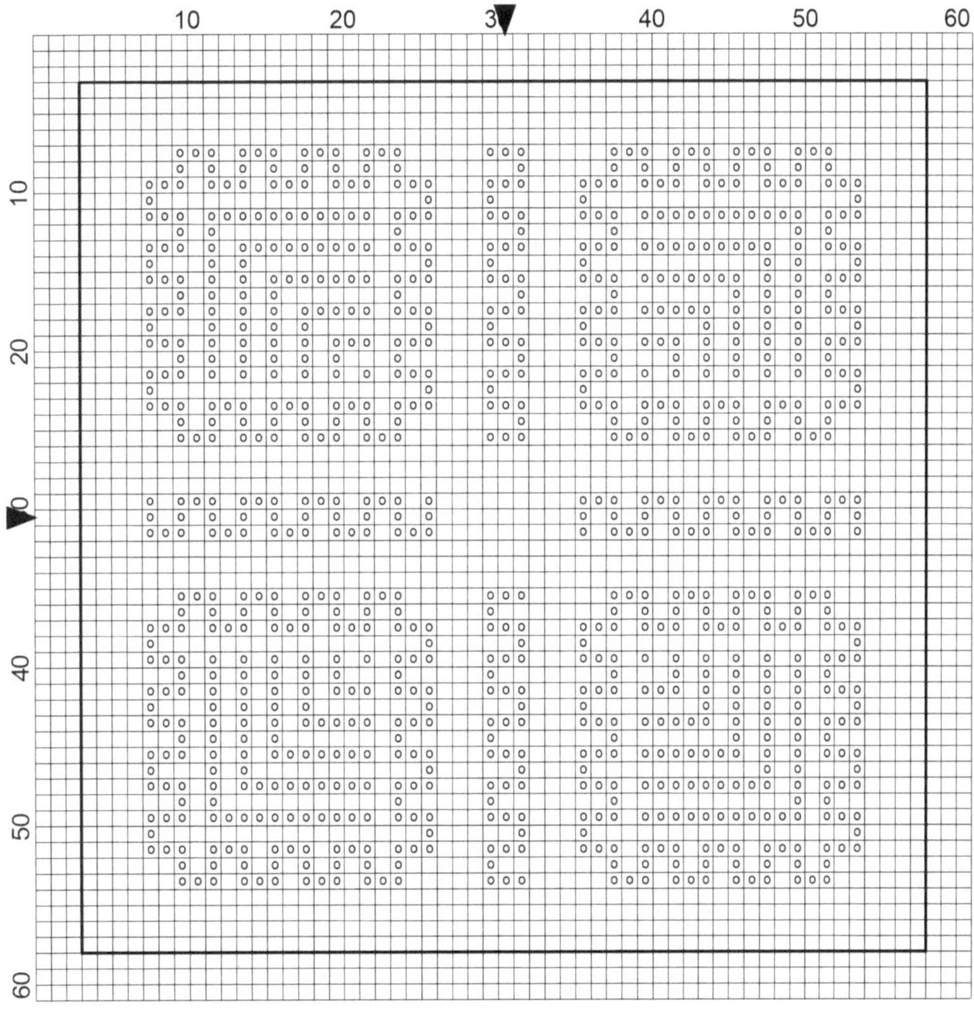

BEGINNER'S BISCORNU
with felt base.

Construction - The outer line on the graph is the **fold line** for the top of the pincushion. Backstitch this line with two strands of thread. When all the cross stitching is complete, fold the fabric, along this line, to the wrong side and tack down with large stitches.

To give the top of the pincushion a smooth finish, a piece of batting or felt can be placed on the wrong side of the cross stitch before folding over. This step is optional.

Cut a square of felt to the same size as the top - **ie with hems included.**

Hem the square of felt as you did with the cross stitch fabric so that both squares are now exactly the same size. Mark the midpoint of each square with a pin.

Continue to construct the felt base biscornu in exactly the same way as with the fabric pincushion following the instructions from pages 16 - 18.

Once again stitched in different colours and using other felt options the pincushions look very different.

All the biscornu pincushions in this book are made with either a cross sitch fabric base, a fabric base or a felt base, as described in the last few pages.

These instructions will be referred to for the construction of each biscornu in the book.

CATS BISCORNU

CATS BISCORNU

Design Size: 4.5" (11cms) square

Stitch Count: 57sts square

Fabric: 25 count Antique White Lugana for the top (20cms Square)
25 count Vintage Grey Lugana for the base (20 cms square)
Batting or felt which is optional
Black button
Stuffing of your choice

DMC threads: * 310 Black

The eyes are cross stitched with two strands of thread over two strands of fabric.
Use one strand of black for all the backstitching except for the outer fold line on both pieces of fabric. Use two strands for this.

Backstitch a 57 stitch square on the Vintage Grey Lugana. This will be the same size as the outer backstitched fold line, that surrounds the cats on the top of the pincushion.
The base is not cross stitched.

For the construction of the biscornu pincushion refer to pages 11 - 12

CATS BISCORNU

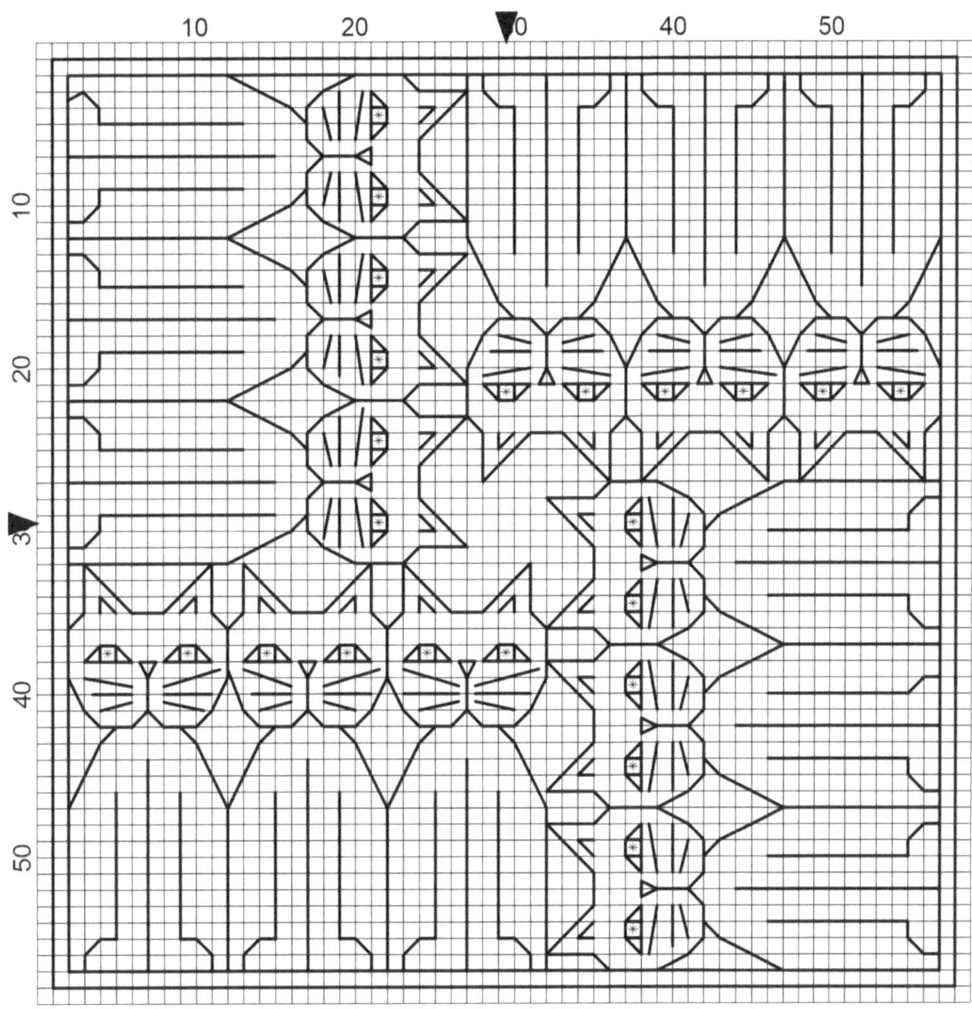

COFFEE BISCORNU

Design Size: 4.5" (11cms) square

Stitch Count: 58sts square

Fabric: 25 count Antique White Lugana for the top
25 count Lugana in your chosen colour for the base
Batting or felt which is optional
Stuffing of your choice
Brown button or miniature coffee cup

DMC threads:	x	838	Beige Brown - vy dk
	o	839	Beige Brown - dk
	.	841	Beige Brown - lt

The design is cross stitched and backstitched with two strands of thread over two strands of 25 count Lugana fabric.
Backstitch the outer fold lines with two strands of 839.

For the construction of the biscornu pincushion refer to pages 11 - 12.

COFFEE BISCORNU

COFFEE BISCORNU

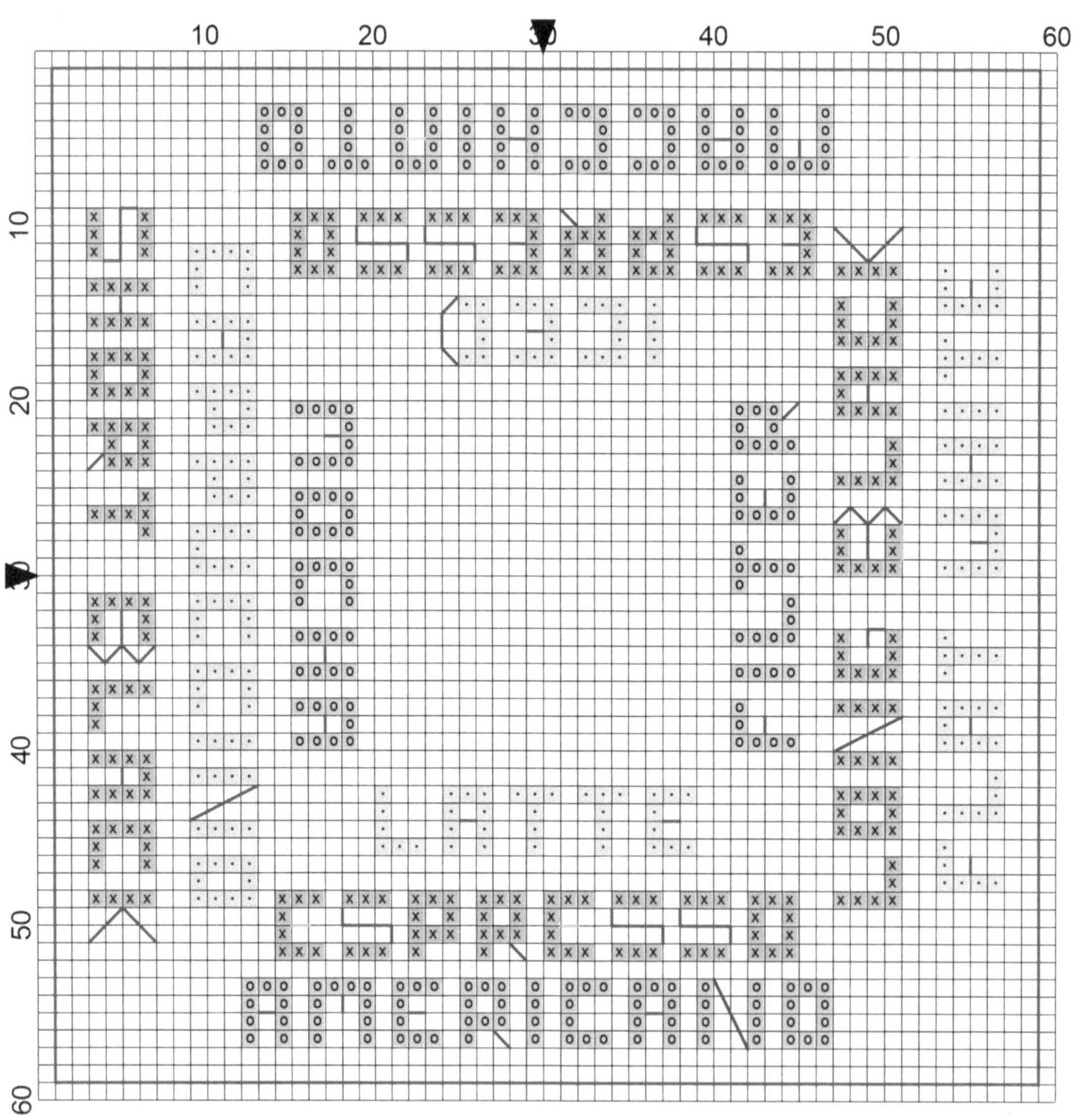

COFFEE BISCORNU

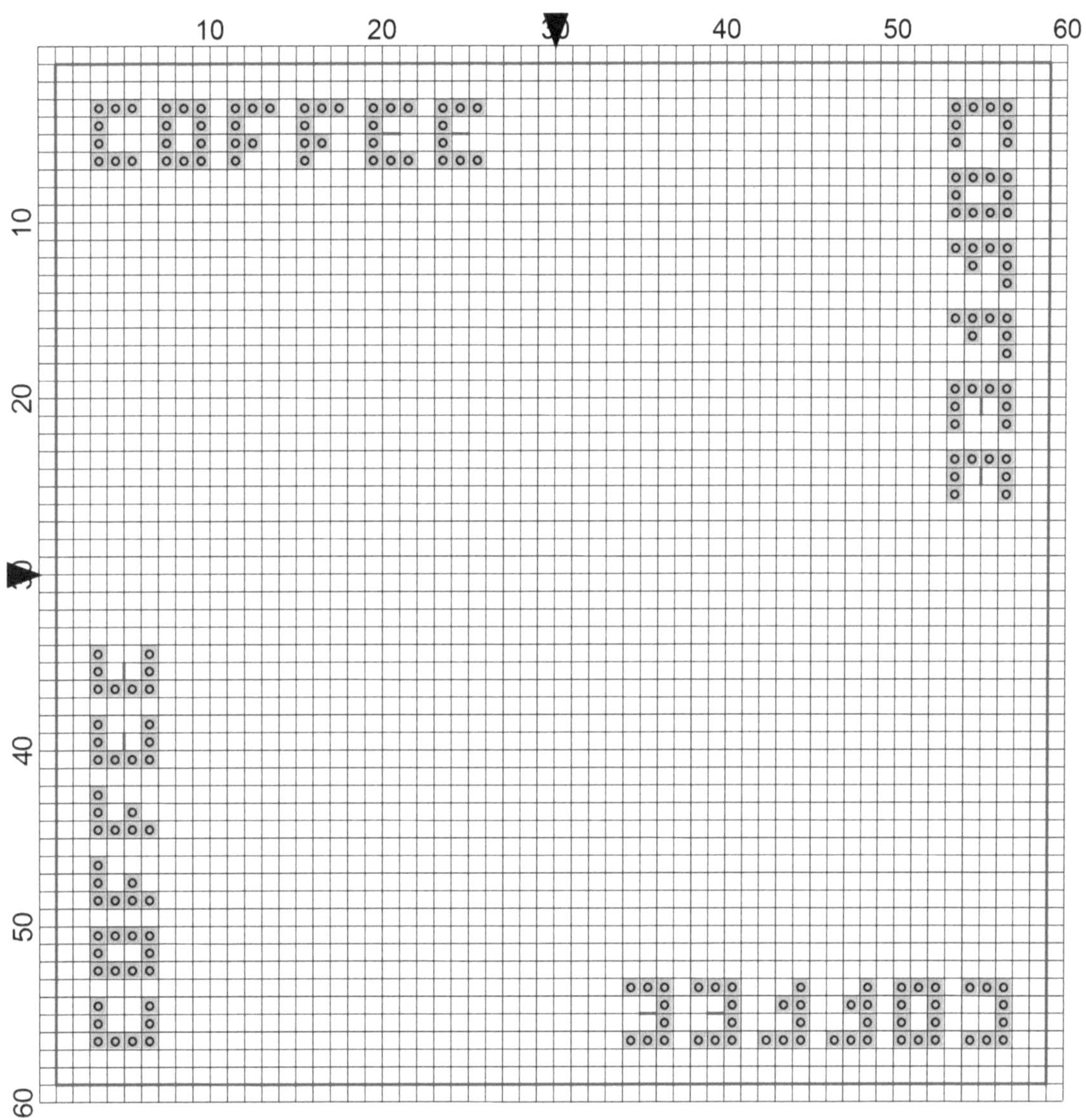

COFFEE BISCORNU

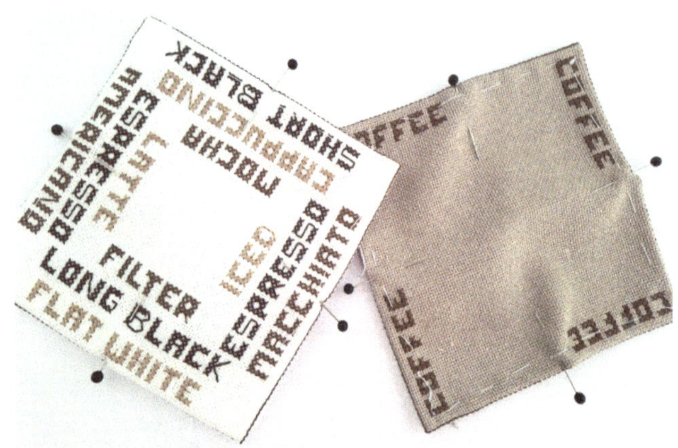

CHERRY BISCORNU

CHERRY BISCORNU

Design Size: 4.5" (11cms) square

Stitch Count: 35 sts square (stitched in a diamond rather than a square)

Fabric: 25 count White Lugana for the top - 25 cms square
Cherry themed patchwork fabric
Batting or felt which is optional
Stuffing of your choice
Cherry Button

DMC threads:

bs	310	Black
o	815	Garnet - med
-	816	Garnet
l	935	Avocado Green - dk
x	937	Avocado Green

Breaking all the rules of cross stitch this is the easiest way to stitch this pincushion.

The golden rule of cross stitch is to have all the stitches lying in the same direction. That is all the lower stitches sloping the same way and all those crossing on the top, laying in the opposite direction.

This is a pincushion that will be used often - not a family heirloom to be handed down from one generation to another. I wanted to stitch it as quickly and as easily as possible.

To keep the cherries coming from each corner the stitching is done in the ' V ' of the square. Picture the stitching in a diamond rather than a square. A square tipped on its side. Take a look at the graph and it will all become clear.

I have stitched one corner, then turned the fabric and stitched the next one in the next 'V' so that the bottom o f the 'V' is pointing to me each time.

So......the rule has been broken in that across the whole design the stitches do not all sit the same way.

It doesn't matter!! The pincushion is twisted when it is sewn together and no one will know. It is the easiest and quickest way to stitch this useful little pincushion.

Don't stitch that way when working on a flat piece as it will be very obvious, but for this it is perfect.

The design is stitched using two strands of thread over two strands of fabric.

Begin by backstitching the border on the cross stitch fabric - 35 stitches on each side of the diamond shape. This is also the fold line.

Work the cherries in each corner as described, backstitching the cherries with one strand of 815, the leaves with one strand of 935 and the stalks with two strands of 935.

For the construction of the pincushion refer to pages 16 - 18.

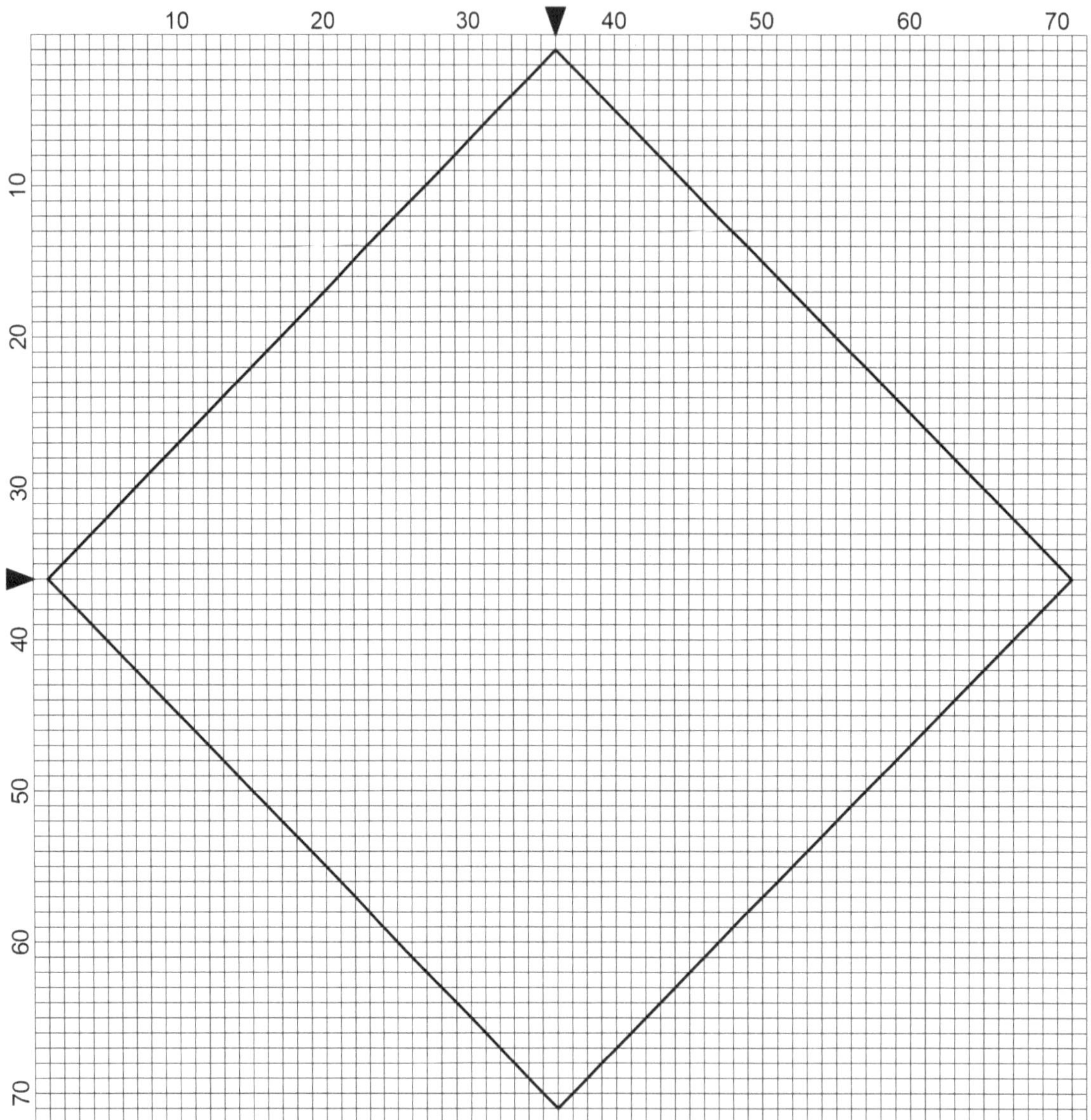
10
20
30
40
50
60
70
10
20
30
40
50
60
70

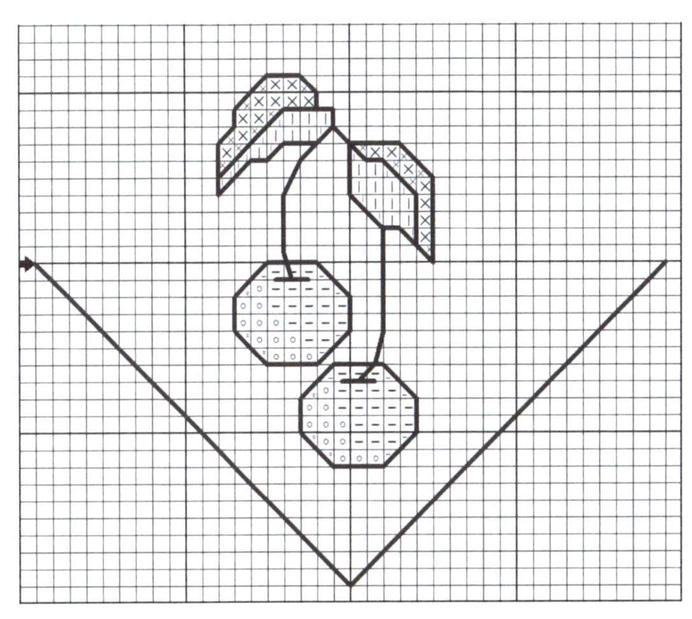

HOUSES BISCORNU

Design Size: 4.5" (11cms) square

Stitch Count: 60sts square

Fabric: 25 count Antique White Lugana for the top (20cms square)
25 count Red Lugana for the base (20 cms square)
Batting or felt which is optional
Red button
Stuffing of your choice

DMC threads: 310 Black
498 Christmas Red

Use two strands of black for all the backstitching except when backstitching the post box. Use one strand of black for this. Cross stitch the post box with two strands of red.
When backstitching around the outer, fold line for the top of the pincushion use two strands of 498.

Backstitch around a 60 stitch square on the Red Lugana using two strands of 498.

This will be the same size as the outer red backstitched fold line that surrounds the houses on the top of the pincushion. The base is not cross stitched.

Complete the Houses biscornu following the instructions on pages 11 - 12.

HOUSES BISCORNU

HOUSES BISCORNU

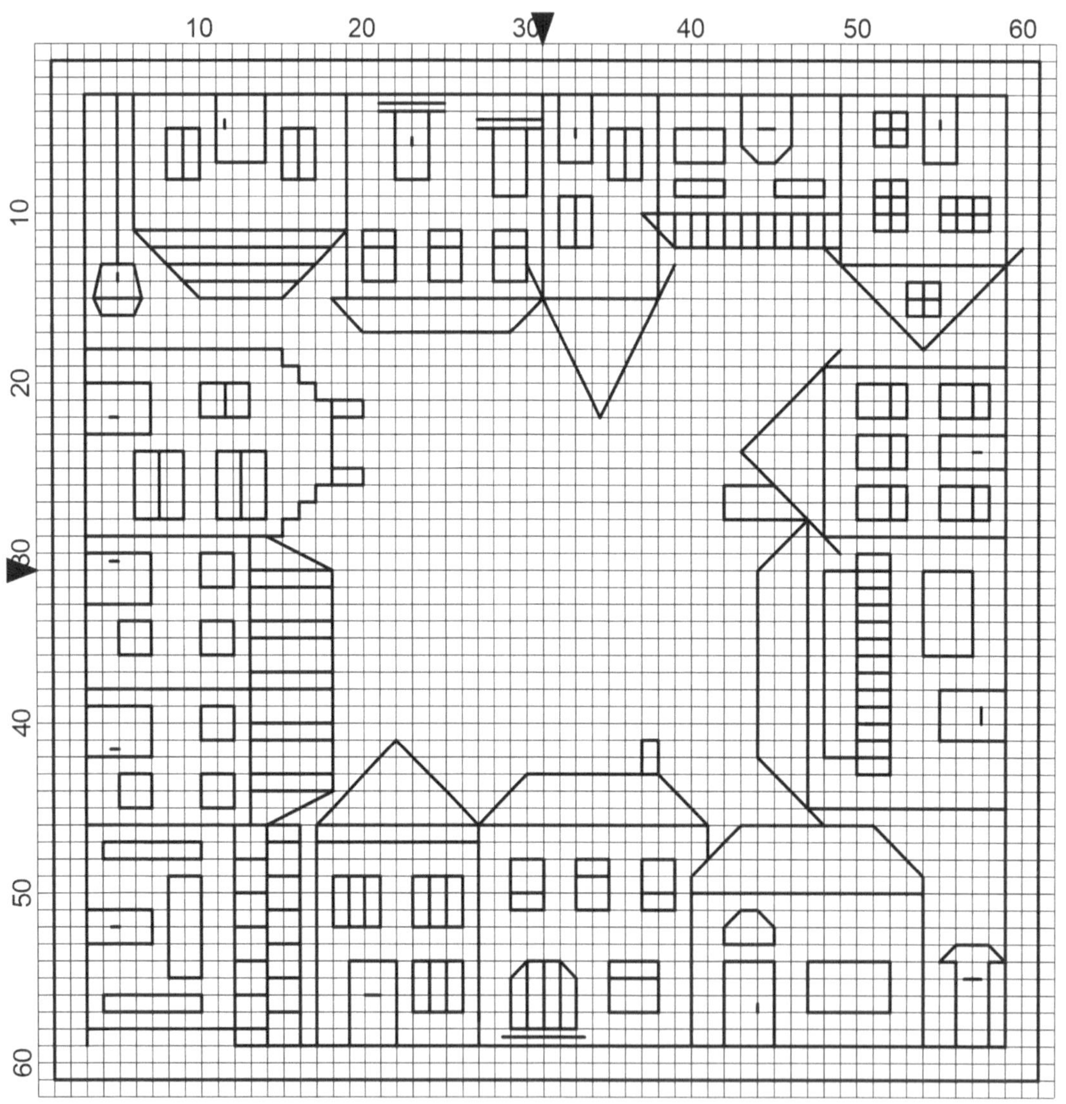

OWLS BISCORNU

OWLS BISCORNU
(black or brown)

Design Size: 4" (10cms) square

Stitch Count: 52 sts square

Fabric: 25 count Bone Lugana for the top (for the brown owls)
25 count White Lugana for the top (for the black owls)
Owl print patchwork fabric for the bases
Batting or felt which is optional
Black or brown button
Stuffing of your choice

DMC threads: Black thread for the black version and any Brown that matches your fabric for the base.

The eyes are cross stitched with two strands of black/brown thread over two strands of fabric. Use one strand of black to backstitch the eyes and depending on your preference use one or strands of black/brown to backstitch the owls.

Use two strands of your chosen colour to backstitch the outer, fold line.

Complete the Owl pincushion by following the instructions on pages 16 - 18.

OWLS BISCORNU

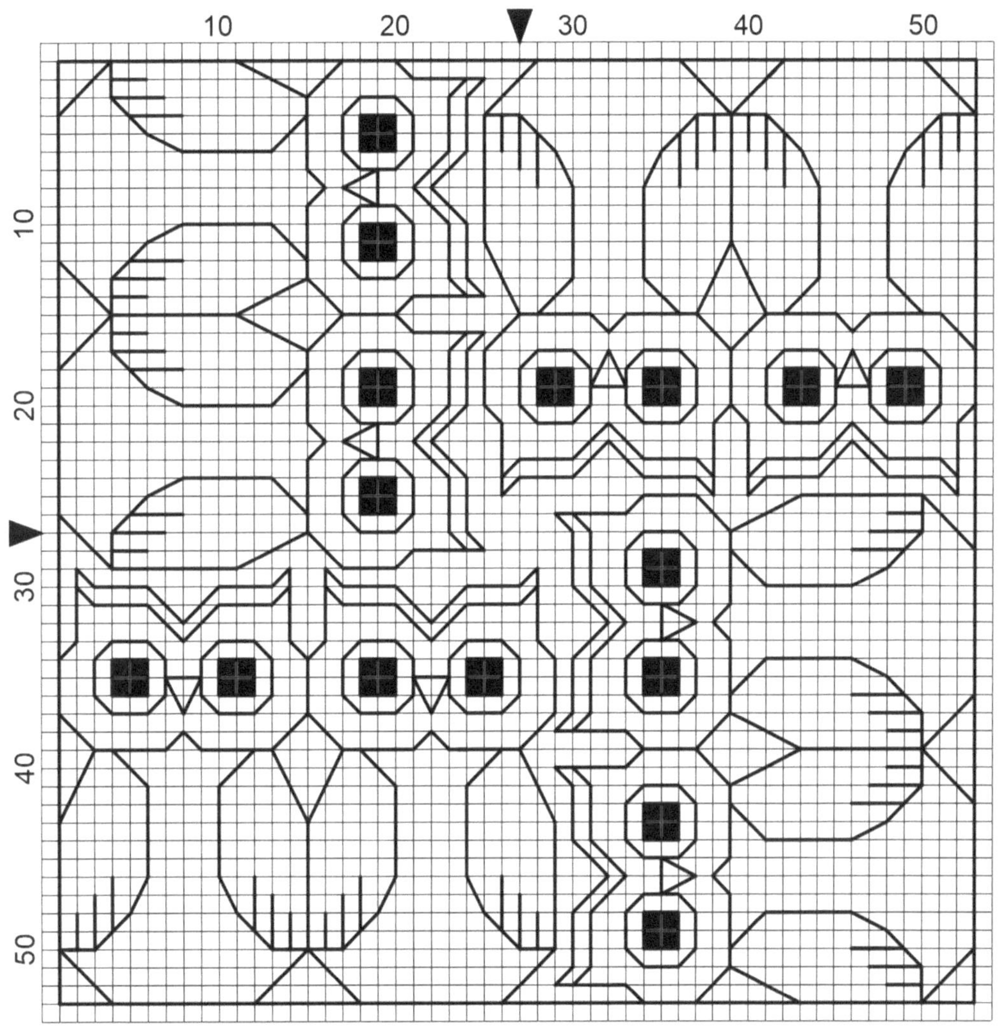

ROSES and RIBBONS BISCORNU

Design Size: 4" (10cms) square

Stitch Count: 52 sts square

Fabric: 25 count White Lugana for the top
Wool blend felt for the base
Batting or felt which is optional

Embellishments: 3 small lace flowers half an inch in diameter
3 small pink ribbon roses
Ribbon to match floss - a liitle over half an inch wide
Stuffing of your choice

The DMC thread list can be found on the following page.

The design is cross stitched with two strands of thread over two strands of 25 count Lugana fabric. The blank areas on the graph are where the ribbon is slip stitched in place. Small lace flowers are sewn in the area stitched in 3032 - see the photograph.

Complete as per the instructions on page 22 for the felt base. After the indentation has been made in the centre, glue three small ribbon roses in the hollow.

ROSES and RIBBONS BISCORNU

ROSES and RIBBONS BISCORNU

DMC threads:

Symbol	Number	Colour
·		Ecru
l	316	Antique Mauve
x	3032	Mocha Brown
y	3713	Salmon
/	3781	Mocha Brown - dk
o	3803	Mauve
s	Ecru 316	One strand of each colour worked together
c	Ecru 3803	One strand of each colour worked together
*	4504	Hydrangea - DMC Coloris

ROSES and RIBBONS BISCORNU

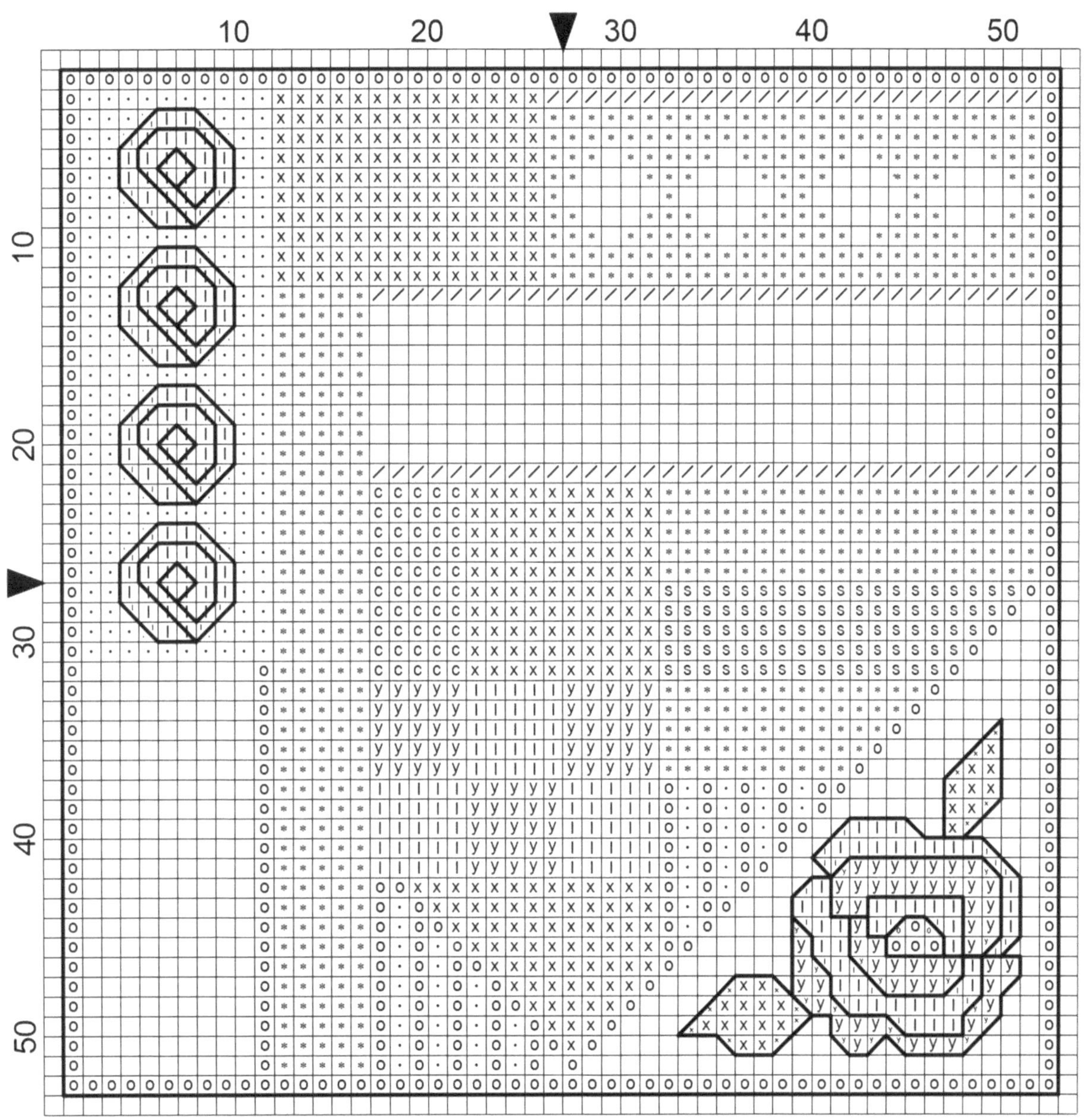

SHEEP BISCORNU

Design Size: 4.75" (12cms) square

Stitch Count: 60 sts square

Fabric: 25 count White Lugana for the top
25 count Pale Green Lugana for the base
(This is my first attempt at dyeing fabric. I wet a piece of white Lugana and painted it with diluted green dye).
Batting or felt which is optional
Black button
Stuffing of your choice

DMC threads: 03 Tin Grey
310 Black

Use one strand of black for all the backstitching except for the outer backstitched fold line on both pieces of fabric. Use two strands for this.

Use two strands of DMC 03 Tin Grey for the black sheep's ears, face and legs.
The base is not cross stitched.

Complete the pincushion following the instructions on pages 11 - 12.

SHEEP BISCORNU

SHEEP BISCORNU

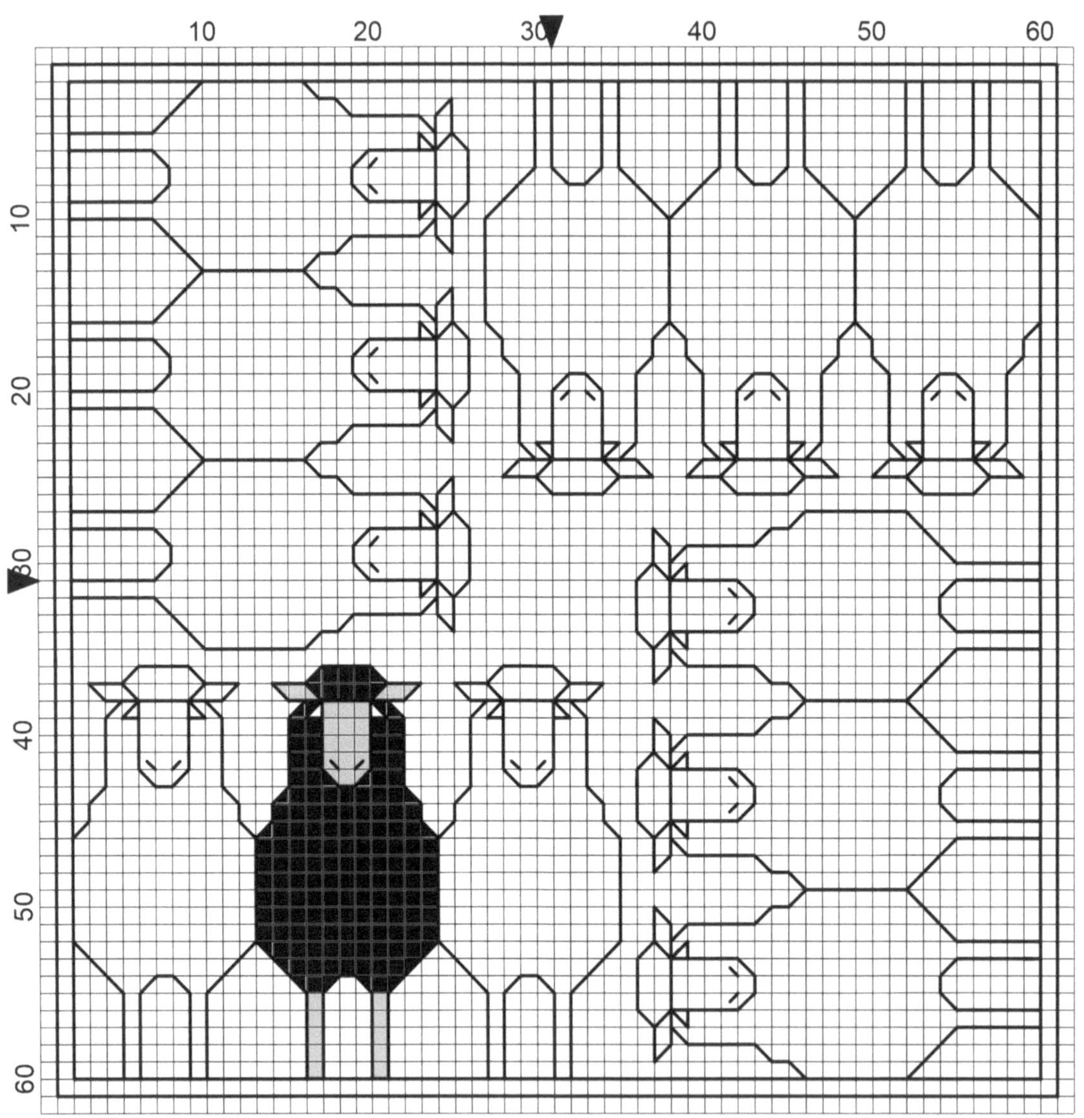

POPPY BISCORNU

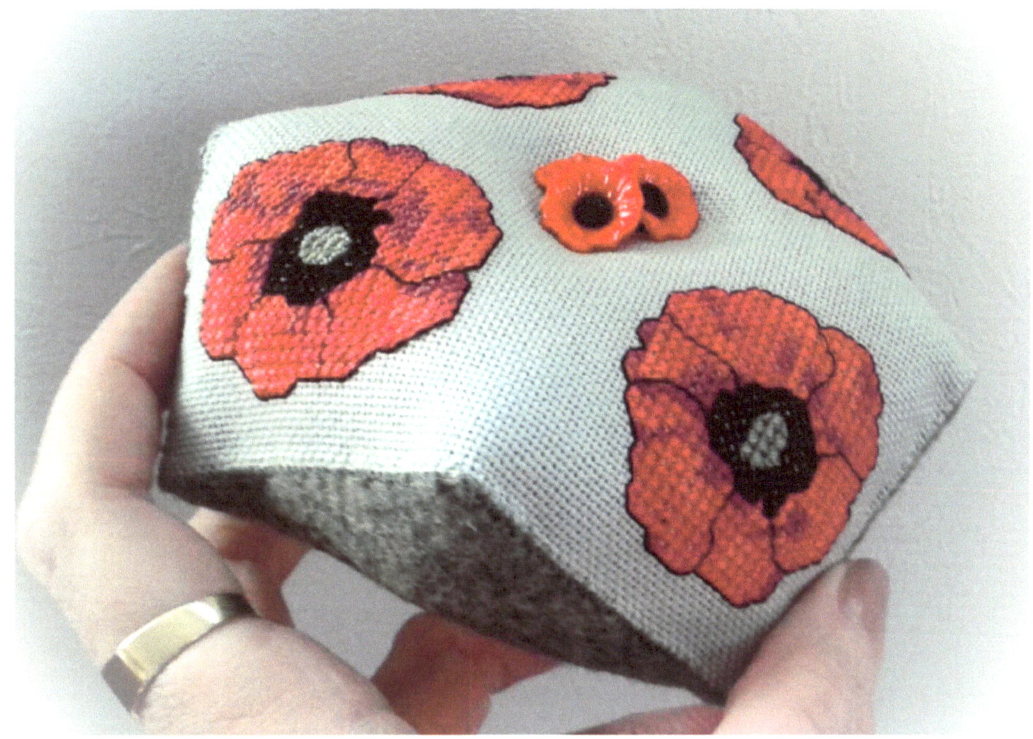

POPPY BISCORNU

Design Size: 4.75"(12cms) square

Stitch Count: 62 sts square

Fabric: 25 count Moss Green Lugana for the top
Moss Green coloured felt for the base
Three poppy buttons
Stuffing of your choice

DMC threads:

Symbol	DMC	Colour
o	310	Black
/	522	Fern Green
.	4205	Caliente - DMC Variations

The design is cross stitched with two strands of thread over two strands of Lugana fabric.

Work each stitch of the Variations thread individually for continuity of colour. It is often better to work in small blocks than in rows to prevent getting a striped effect. Backstitch the poppies with one strand of black. The outer fold line is backstitched with two strands of 522. Complete the pincushion following the instructions on page 22.

POPPY BISCORNU

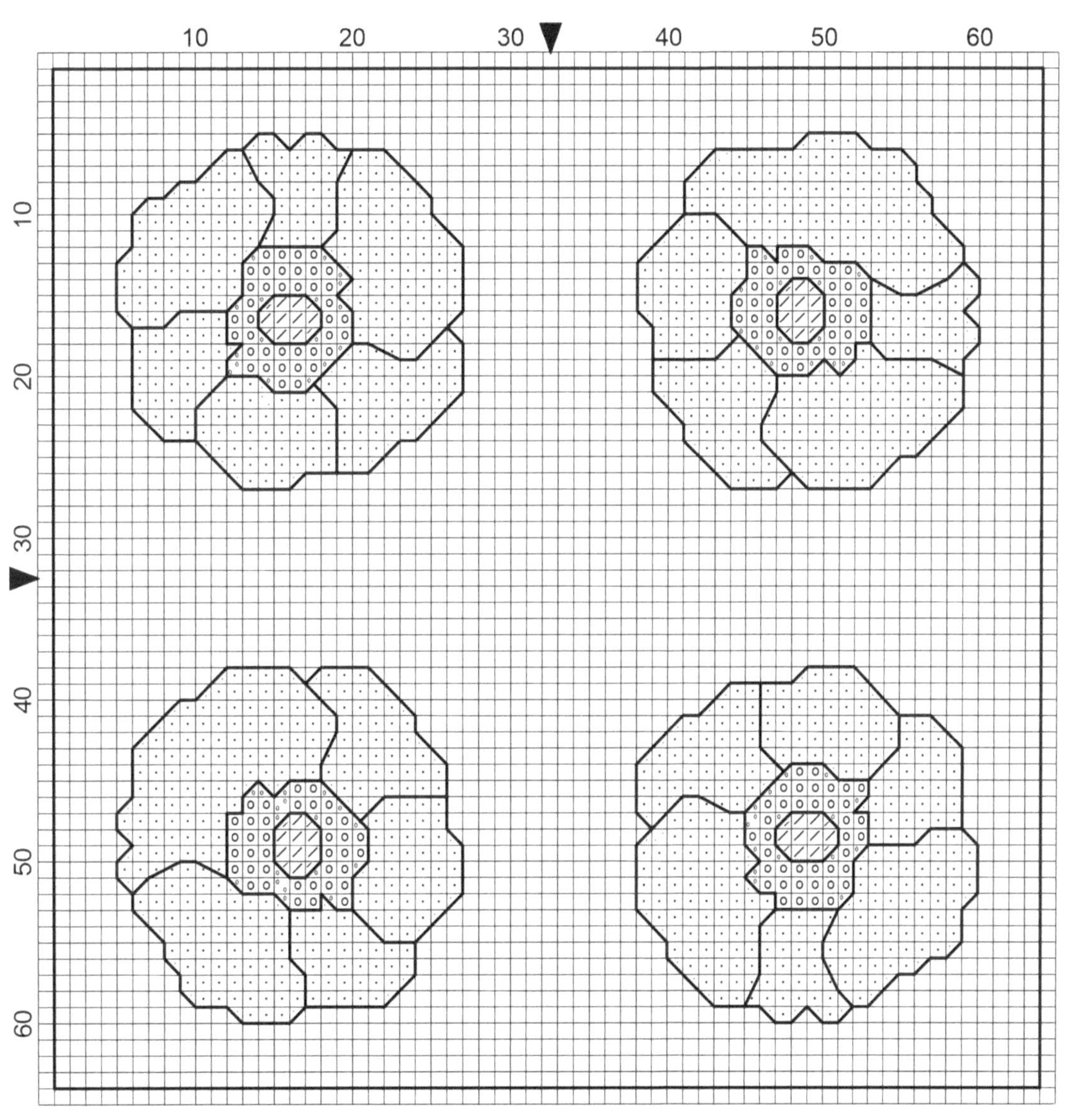

PANSY BISCORNU

Design Size: 4"(10cms) square

Stitch Count: 51 sts square

Fabric: 25 count Pale Lemon Lugana for the top
25 count Bright Pink Lugana for the base both hand dyed by countrystitch.com
One fancy pansy button, brooch or pin
Stuffing of your choice

Threads: x Pansy by Cottage Gardens Threads

The design is cross stitched with two strands of thread over two strands of Lugana fabric.

Work each stitch of the hand dyed thread individually for continuity of colour.
The outer fold line is backstitched with two strands of the Pansy thread.

Complete the pincushion following the instructions on pages 11 - 12.

PANSY BISCORNU

PANSY BISCORNU

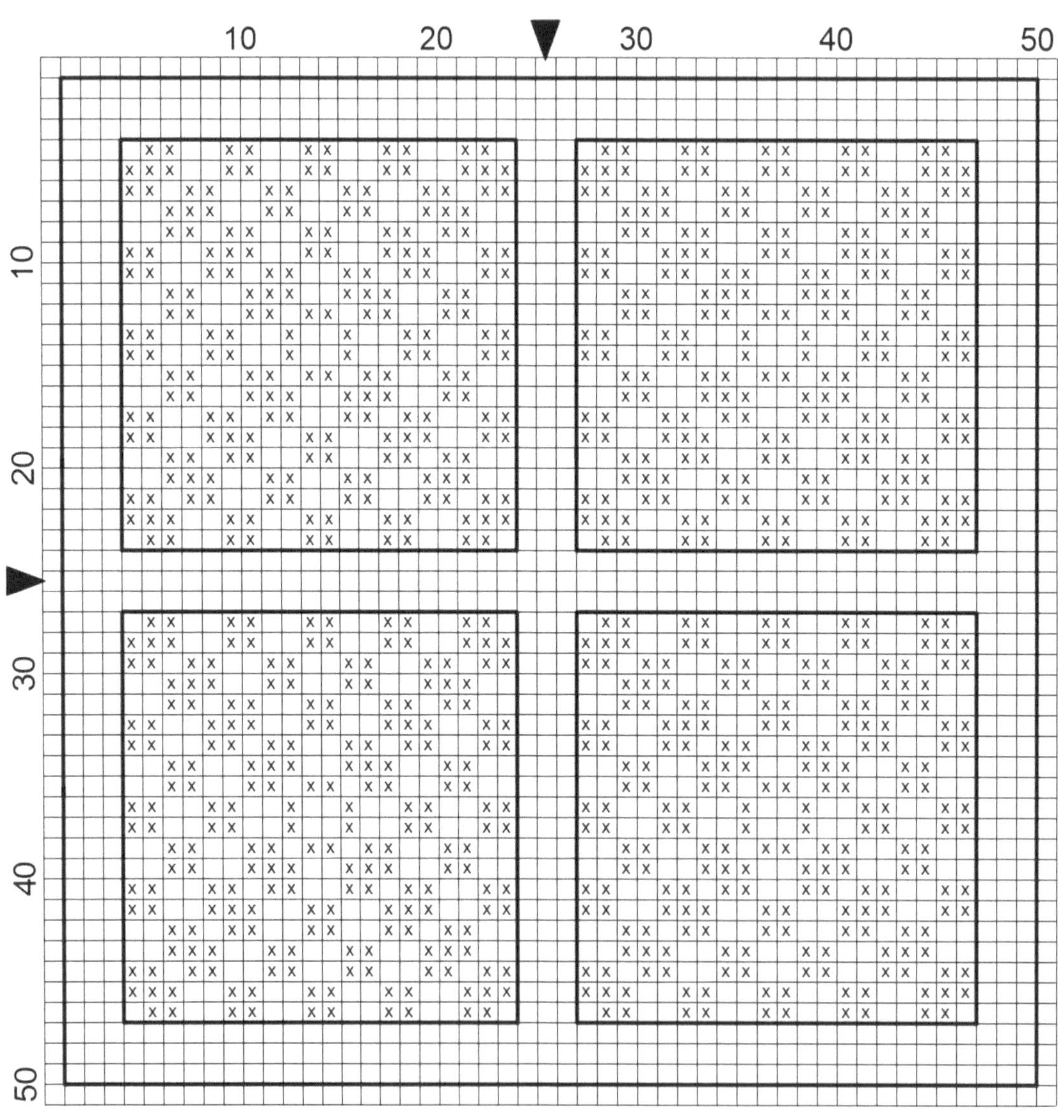

HALLOWEEN BISCORNU

HALLOWEEN BISCORNU

Design Size: 4"(10cms) square

Stitch Count: 52 sts square

Fabric: 25 count marbled Vintage Grey Lugana for the top and base
Three pumpkin buttons
Batting or felt which is optional
Stuffing of your choice

Extras: Tiny charms (nail art charms are ideal), small black ribbon roses and leaves, tiny buttons, lace flowers or bits and bobs from your stash.

DMC threads:

Symbol	DMC	Colour
.		White
-	04	Tin
x	310	Black
bs	535	Ash Grey
o	4124	Bonfire - DMC Variations

The design is cross stitched with two strands of thread over two strands of Lugana fabric.

The outer fold line for both the top and the base are backstitched with two strands of 310. TRICK or TREAT on the base is cross stitched with two strands of 310.

Complete the pincushion using the instructions on pages 11 - 12.

HALLOWEEN BISCORNU

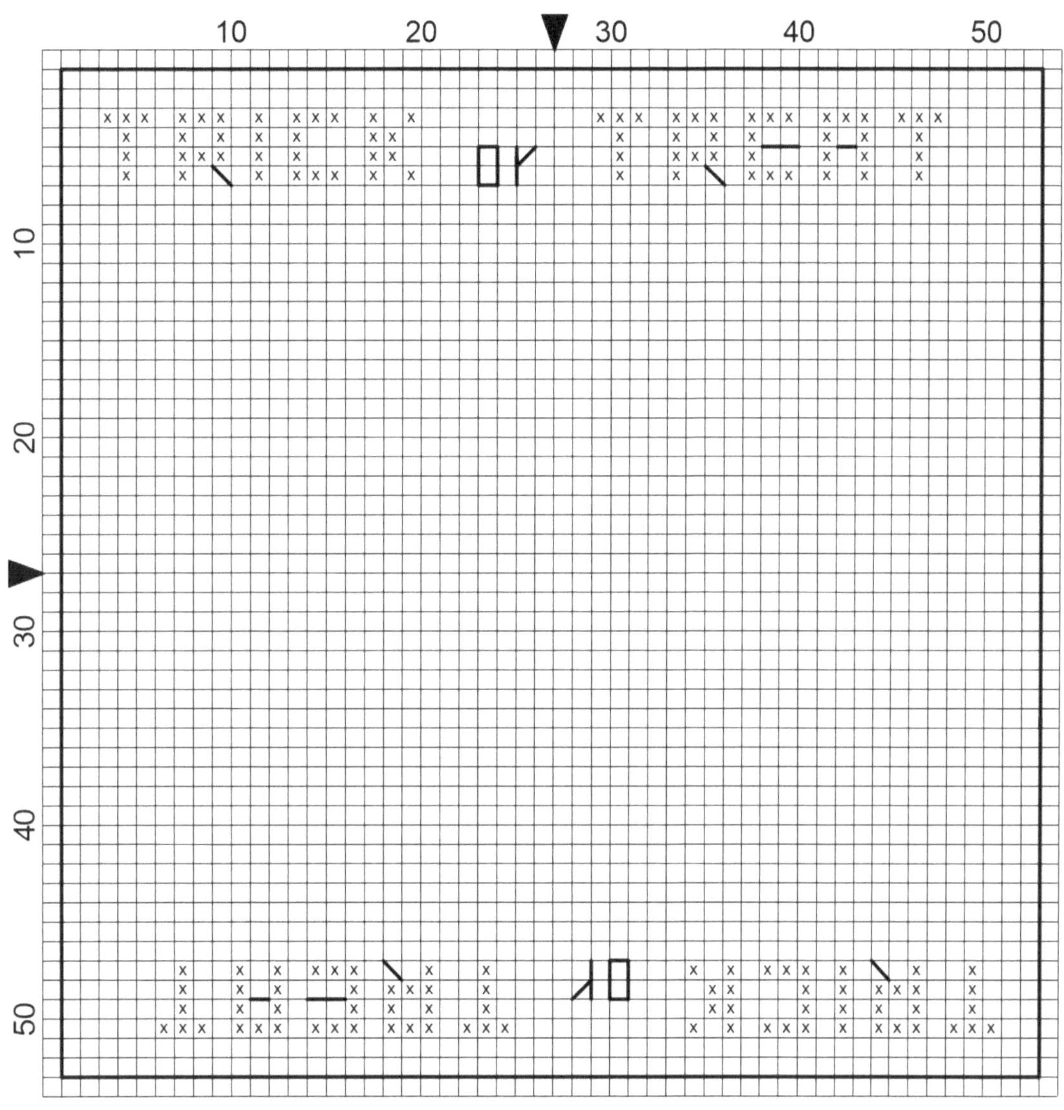

HALLOWEEN BISCORNU

The design for the top of the Hallween biscornu is cross stitched with two strands of thread over two strands of 25 count Lugana fabric.

When stitching with DMC Variations complete each cross stitch as you go to get continuity of colour.

Pumpkin - Backstitch with one strand of 310.

Gravestone - Backstitch with one strand of 535.

Ghost and 'B' of BOO - Backstitch with one strand of 310 and work two tiny French knots for the eyes. Backstitch the rectangles around the ghost and gravestone with one strand of 04.

Skulls - Backstitch with one strand of 04.

Spider's web - Backstitch with one strand of 310.

'TREAT' - Backstitch with one strand of 310.

HALLOWEEN BISCORNU

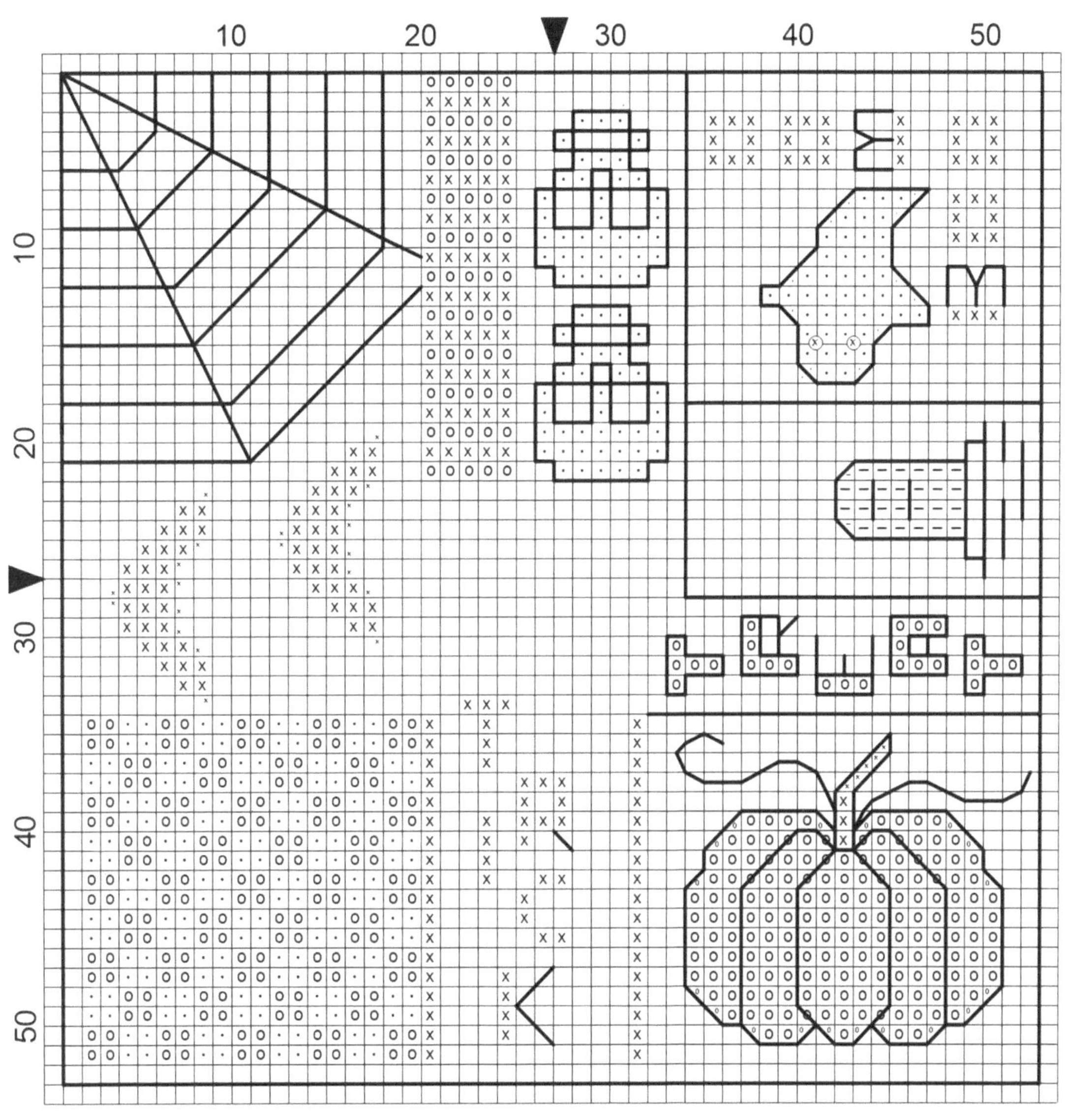

ROSE BUSH BISCORNU

Design Size : Bottom pincushion - 8cms
Third pincushion - 7cms
Second pincushion - 6cms
Top pincushion - 5cms

Stitch Count: Bottom pincushion - 40 sts square
Third pincushion - 35 sts square
Second pincushion - 30 sts square
Top pincushion - 25 sts square

Fabric: 25 count White, Ash Rose and Maize Lugana
Three small ribbon roses for the centre of the top pincushion
Stuffing of your choice

Threads:

bs	223	Shell Pink
bs	351	Coral
bs	744	Yellow
Lazy Daisy	3053	Green Grey
bs	3727	Antique Mauve
bs	3731	Dusty Rose
x	4090	DMC Variations - Golden Oasis
.	4150	DMC Variations - Desert Sand
o	4170	DMC Variations - Whispering Wind

ROSE BUSH BISCORNU

ROSE BUSH BISCORNU

The design is cross stitched with two strands of thread over two strands of Lugana fabric.

Work each stitch of the Variations thread individually for continuity of colour.

Backstitch the 4090 rose with one strand of 351, the 4150 rose with one strand of 223 and the 4170 rose with one strand of 3731.

The 40st square and the 30st square outer fold lines are backstitched with two strands of 3727.
The 35st square and the 25st square outer fold lines are backstitched with two strands of 744. Work random lazy daisy stitches for leaves with two strands of 3053.
More photos are on page 66.
Work the same design in each square regardless of size except for the smallest pincushion.
Complete each biscornu following the instructions on pages 11 - 12.

When indenting the pincushions take the extra long needle through all the pincushions and back again to secure.

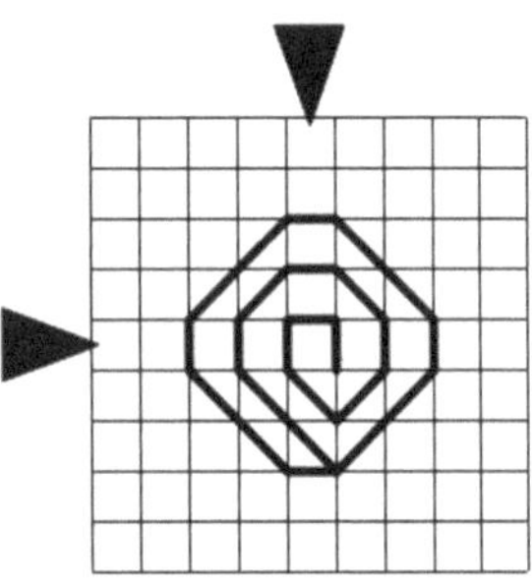

backstitch detail for
each rose

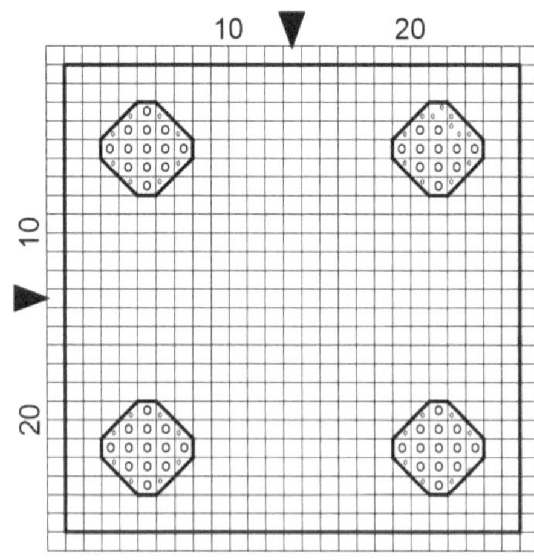

top pincushion top

ROSE BUSH BISCORNU

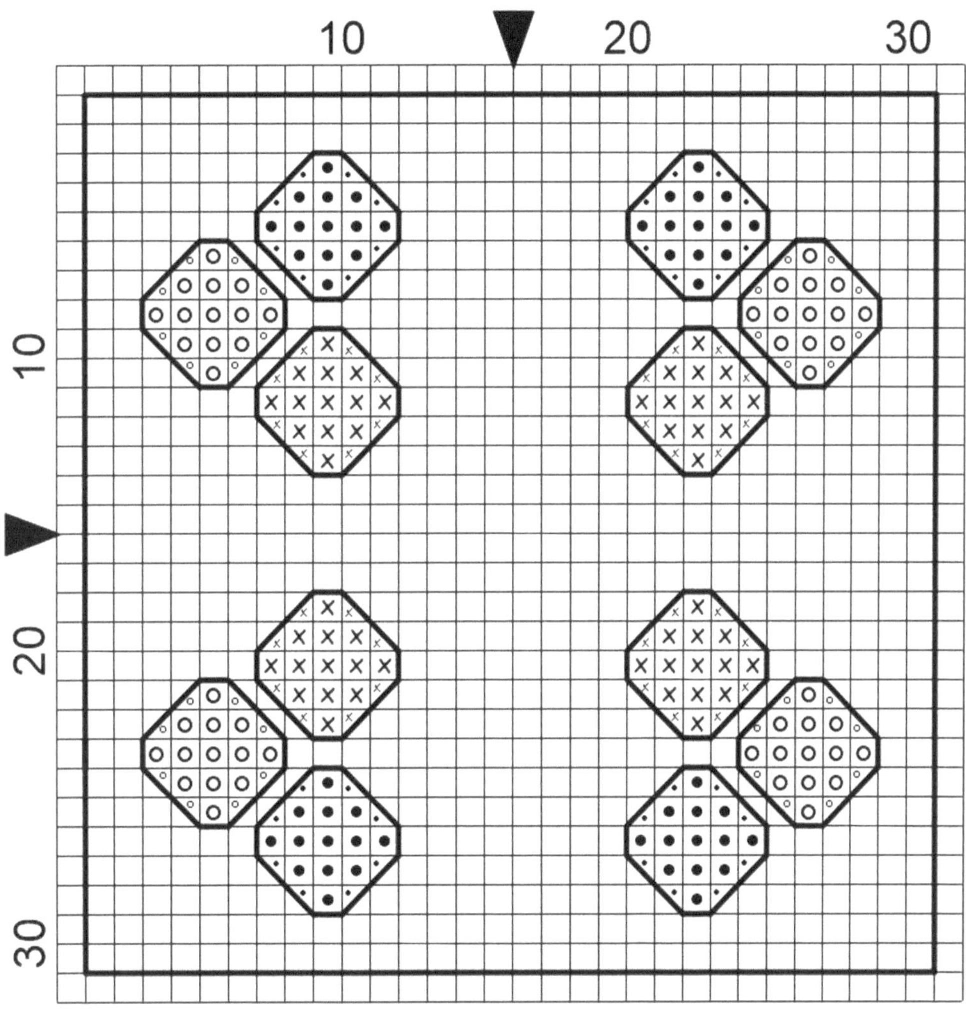

WASTE NOT WANT NOT BISCORNU

The next three biscornu pincushions don't really need a pattern. Once you get started you can simply keep stitching, all the while using up your leftover threads.

Waste Not Want Not came about while I was stitching a large project with a lot of colours. When I couldn't be bothered winding thread back on the bobbin I stitched row after row around a centre square and yet another pincushion emerged.

WASTE NOT WANT NOT BISCORNU

Design Size: 4" (10cms) square

Stitch Count: 52 sts square

Fabric: 25 count Lugana in any colour for the top square
25 count Lugana in a colour to match one of the cottons used in the top.
One button
Stuffing of your choice

Threads: Lengths of left over threads

The design is cross stitched with two strands of thread over two strands of Lugana fabric. Begin by stitching a four stitch square which will be the centre.

The easiest way to stitch the top of this biscornu, is to stitch in hand and complete each stitch as you go.

Mark the 'top' or 'bottom' of the fabric so you can see where you are when picking the work up to stitch the next colour. Stitch clockwise down one 'side', across the bottom, working the cross stitch as in the photo, working from right to left completing each stitch individually. Then turn the work 90 degrees and continue down the side and across 'the bottom'.

Continue on, using up your ends of cotton until you reach a 50 stitch square.
******** Double check that you have 50 stitches on each side or the biscornu will not work.
Now backstitch 52 sts one row away from the cross stitches all the way around the square, using two strands of thread. Do the same for the base.

Complete the pincushion using the instructions on pages 11 - 12.

WASTE NOT WANT NOT BISCORNU

MINI BISCORNU PINCUSHIONS

Design Size: 2" (5cms)

Stitch Count: 27 sts square

Fabric: 25 count Lugana in any colour for the top and base.
Stuffing of your choice

Threads: One skein of hand dyed or variegated thread

The design is cross stitched with two strands of thread over two strands of Lugana fabric. Begin by stitching a two stitch square which will be the centre.

The easiest way to stitch the top of this biscornu, is to stitch in hand and complete each stitch as you go.

Mark the 'top' or 'bottom' of the fabric so you can see where you are when picking the work up to stitch the next colour. Stitch clockwise down one 'side', across the bottom, working the cross stitch as on Page 67, working from right to left completing each stitch individually. Then turn the work 90 degrees and continue down the side and across 'the bottom'.

Continue on, until you have a square with 25 sts on each side. One stitch away, backstitch a square which will have 27sts on each side. Repeat this 27sts square on a piece of the same fabric for the base.

Complete the pincushion using the instructions on pages 11 - 12.
These minis are not indented.

It is very difficult to stop making these tiny biscornus. There are so many lovely threads to choose from. The options are endless!

MINI BISCORNU PINCUSHIONS

PATCHWORK BISCORNU

This pattern is ideal for using up a length of two strands of stray cotton. In this case the cottons are those not used for the mini biscornus. And a few more that I couldn't resist.

Design Size: 4"(10cms) (stitched in a diamond rather than a square)

Stitch Count: 80 sts square (in a diamond shape)

Fabric: 25 count Lugana in any colour for the top and base.
Stuffing of your choice

Threads: Black and any left over threads.

The design is cross stitched with two strands of thread over two strands of Lugana fabric.

The dark grey squares are stitched in Black.
Backstitch the outer fold line on both the top and the base with two strands of Black.

Complete the pincushion using the instructions on pages 11 - 12.

PATCHWORK BISCORNU

PATCHWORK BISCORNU

Base graph

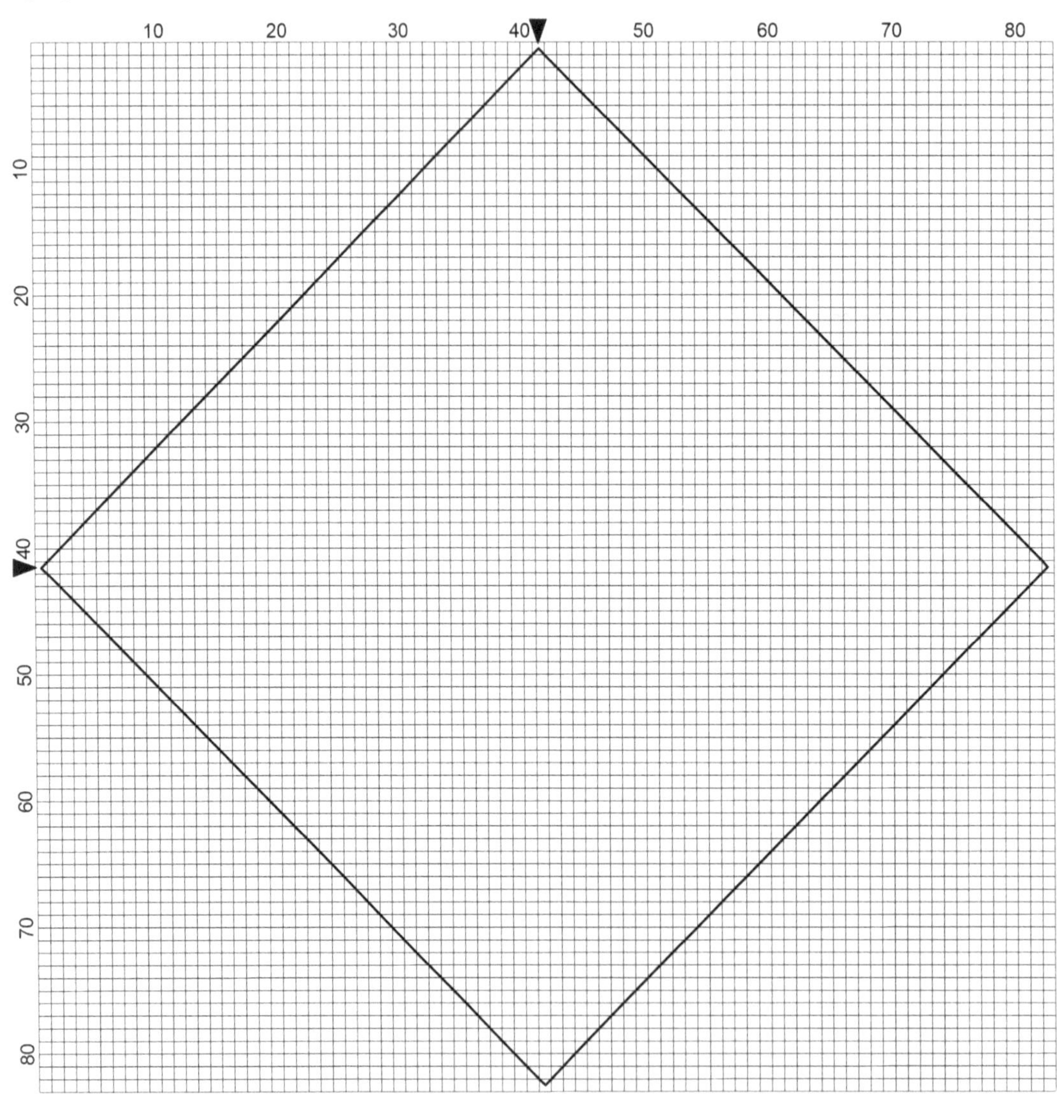

PATCHWORK BISCORNU

Top graph

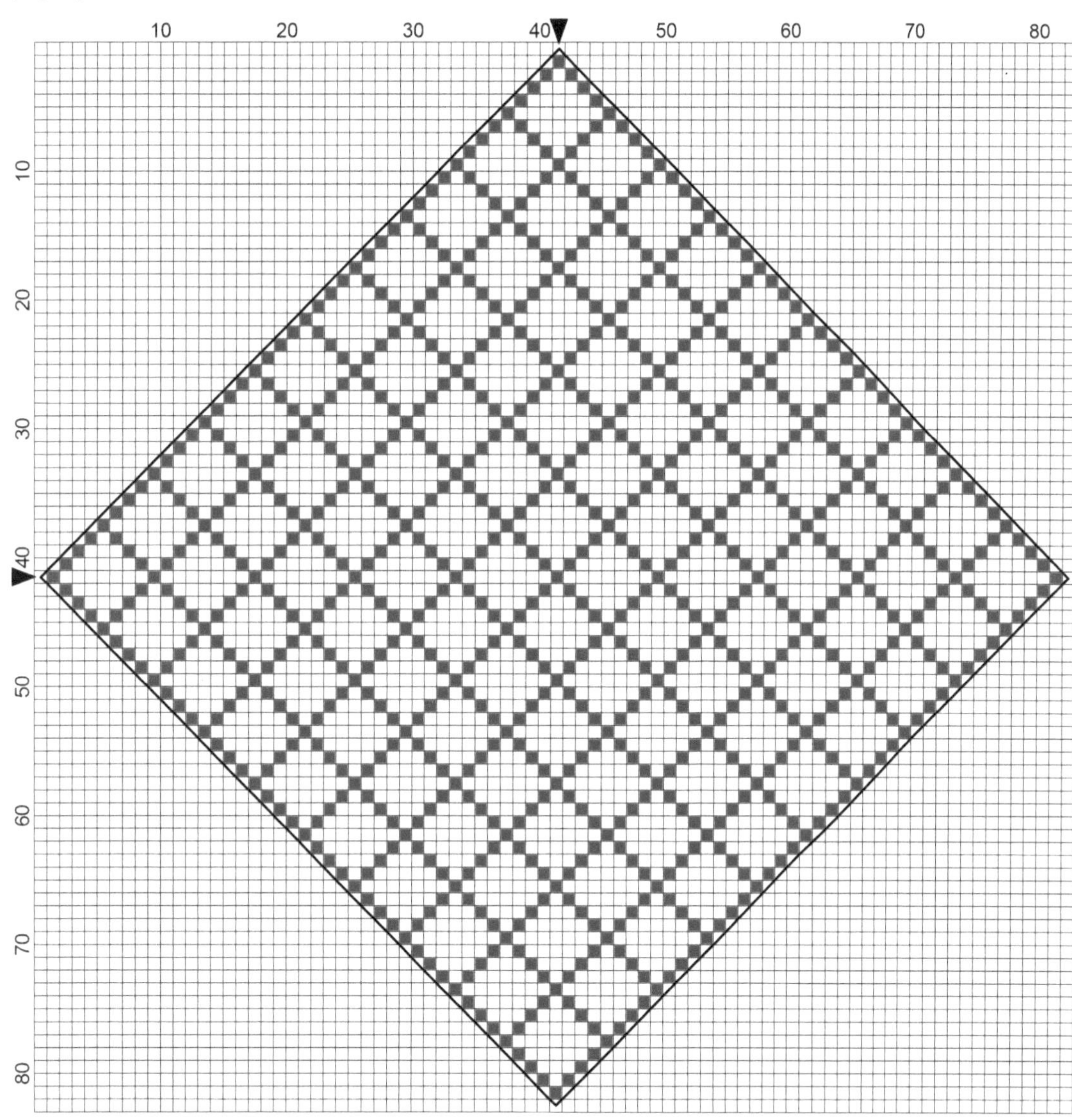

15 SIDED BISCORNU

Another biscornu that is made for using up left over threads and very small pieces of fabric. You can use one piece of fabric to stitch the fifteen squares on or use your scraps.

Design Size: 4"(10cms)

Stitch Count: each square is 20sts

Fabric: I used my favourite 25 count Lugana. Use any cross stitch fabric you have, just be consistent throughout.
Stuffing of your choice

Threads: Whatever colours you want.

The design is cross stitched with two strands of thread over two strands of Lugana fabric.

This is the only Biscornu pincushion in the book that is constructed differently.

Begin with enough scraps of the same cross stitch fabric to stitch 15 squares each with 20 stitches on each side. Leave about 8 stitches between each square as they will all be cut out and folded on the backstitched line.

Backstitch the flowers with one strand of a darker complimentary thread.

The outer fold line is backstitched with two strands of green.

15 SIDED BISCORNU

15 SIDED BISCORNU

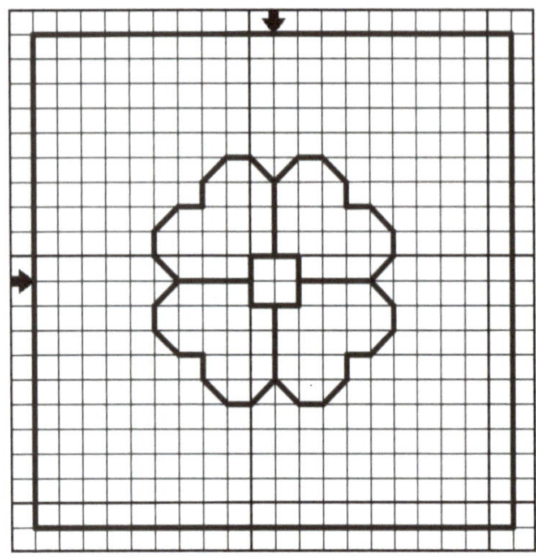

Sew three sides together as in the photo below with a whip stitch, matching each backstitch, stitch for stitch, then add the fifth square (as below) stitching down two sides. This is the top of the pincushion. Sew another 5 squares together in the same way for the bottom.

15 SIDED BISCORNU

Now begin to add the five squares that will make up the middle section.

Stitch each middle section square, beginning at the seam junction of any of the top 5 seams.

Lastly stitch the bottom section of the pincushion beginning as shown above. Keep whip stitching until there are only 3 sides to join. Begin to stuff firmly at this point. Stitch two more sides together leaving just one seam. Add the last little bit of stuffing and close the seam.

Indent the centre as with the other biscornus and stitch some ribbon roses to the top and bottom.

OCTOPUS BISCORNU

The Octopus pincushions are made from scraps of hand dyed fabric and felt that I have had in my stash for ages. Sometimes you keep fabric, as you know that one day a pattern will come along that is just right.

The Blue Octopus began life with a denim head and base but he looked a bit dull. The Black Octopus had a black head and a gold fabric base, but that didn't work either.
Sometimes you need to simply keep trying many options until one looks just right.

They can be any colour - red and grey, pink and purple, orange and brown.
Whatever you are happy with as the octopus is yours and each one will be different.

Design Size: 5"(13cms)

Stitch Count: 70sts

Fabric:

The Blue Octopus
25 count Lugana - mid blue. I used hand dyed 'Raglan Surf' for the top and a piece of fabric from my stash for the base
A piece of dark blue felt for the head

The Black Octopus
25 count Lugana - I used 'Apple Blossom' for the top and the base.
A piece of black or dark grey felt for the head.
Both hand dyed cross stitch fabric came from www.countrystitch.co.nz
Stuffing of your choice

Threads:
DMC 413 for the Black Octopus
DMC 930 for the Blue Octopus

Extras : One pair of 10 - 12mm googly eyes

OCTOPUS BISCORNU

OCTOPUS BISCORNU

The design is cross stitched with two strands of thread over two strands of Lugana fabric.

Backstitch each octopus in the colour used to cross stitch him.

The Head: Cut the head from two pieces of felt from the pattern provided. Using small even stitches, whip stitch around the curved edge leaving the base open.

Whip stitch is simply an over and over stitch, with stitches placed closely together using two strands of matching embroidery thread. The easiest way to do this is to pinch the two outer edges of felt lightly together and taking a very small seam, stitch over and over the edges of the felt, pulling the thread slightly to neaten the stitches.
Turn a little hem towards the inside of the head to give a firm edge to glue the head on. Stuff the head fairly firmly.

Use the instructions on pages 16 - 18 to complete the pincushion.
After the centre has been indented, run a line of glue around the hemline at the base of the head and glue in place. Hold it down firmly with long pins.

When it is thoroughly dry, glue two googly eyes to the head, quite low down near the body.

Your octopus pincushion is now ready to go!

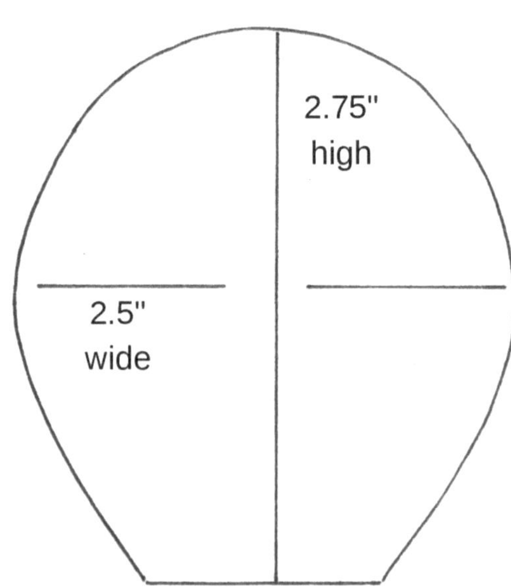

OCTOPUS BISCORNU

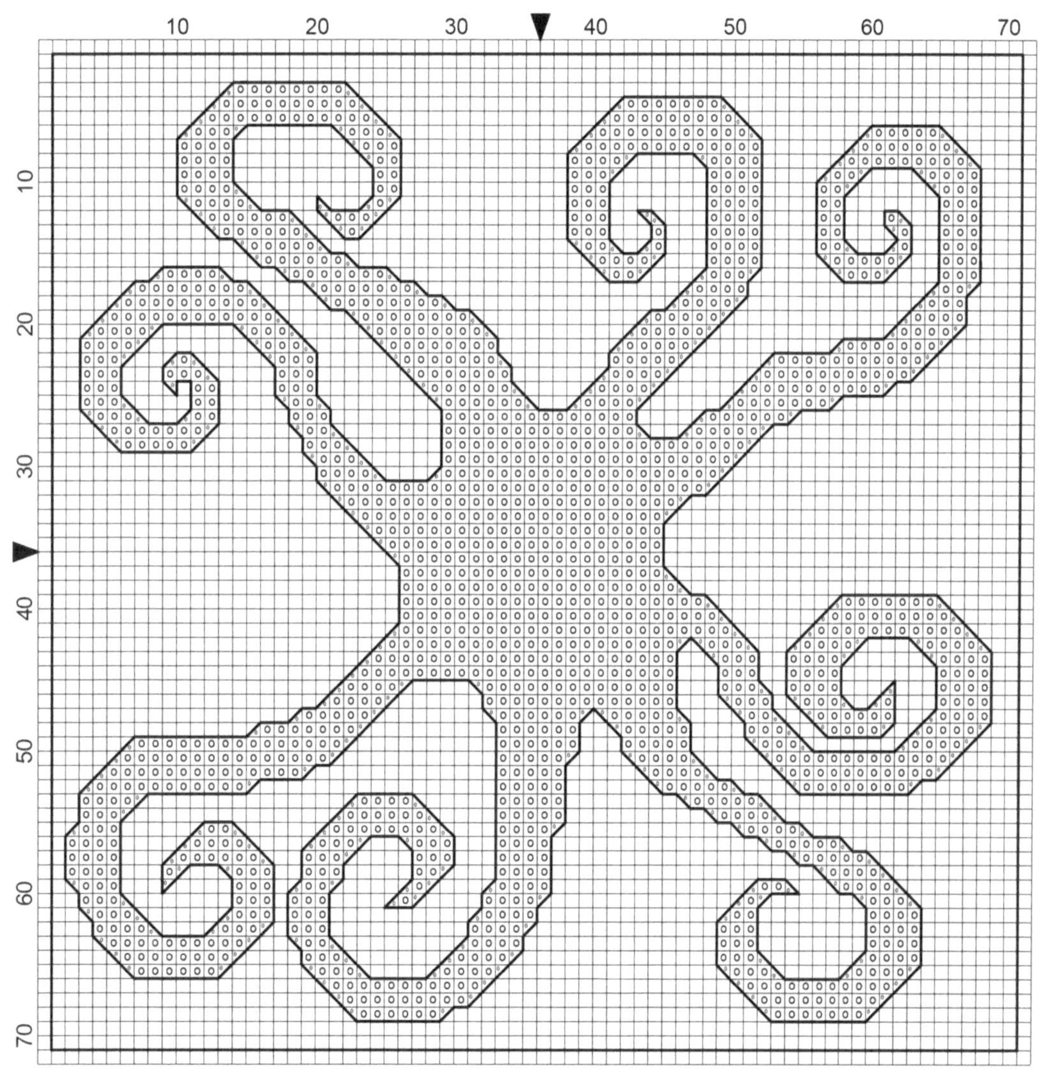

the HOLLY & the IVY
BISCORNU STACK

Design Size :	Bottom pincushion - 8cms Middle pincushion - 7cms Top pincushion - 6cms
Stitch Count:	Bottom pincushion - 40 sts square Middle pincushion - 35 sts square Top pincushion - 30 sts square
Fabric:	25 count White and Moss Green Lugana Stuffing of your choice

Threads:			
	bs	500	Blue Green - vy dk
	bs	4065	DMC Variations Morning Meadow

Embellishments: 3 red beads for the centre of the top pincushion
18 red seed beads

This pattern was originally published in Just CrossStitch magazine in the USA in the Christmas Decorations issue December 2021.

the HOLLY & the IVY
BISCORNU STACK

the HOLLY & the IVY
BISCORNU STACK

The design is stitched with two strands of thread over two strands of fabric. One strand of 500 is used to backstitch the holly and the ivy.
Two strands of DMC Variations is used to backstitch the outer fold lines.

Use the same method of construction as for the Rose Bush pincushion on page 62.

Sew three seed beads between the two leaves of the holly in the corners that have holly.
Stitch or glue three slightly larger red beads at the top of the stack.

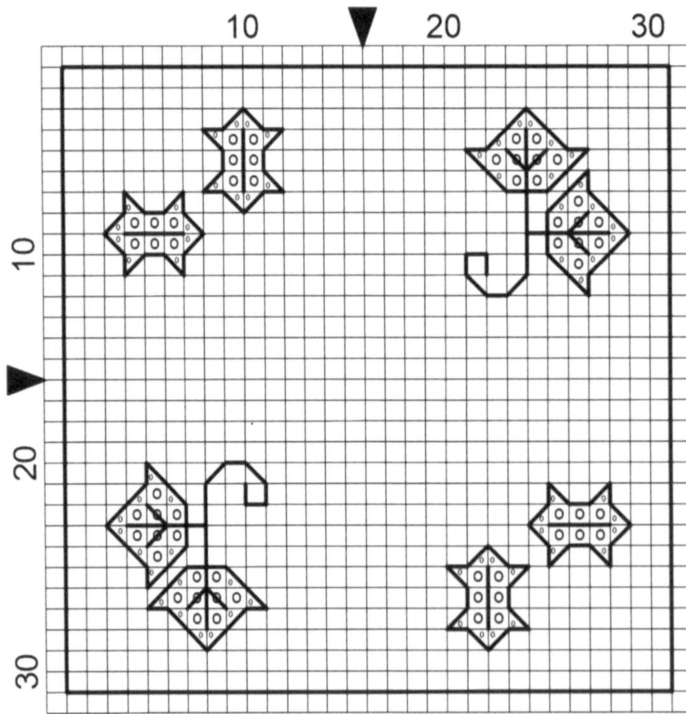

the HOLLY & the IVY
BISCORNU STACK

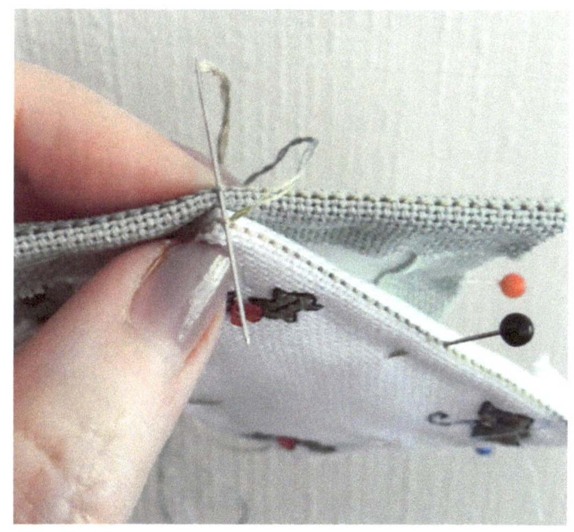

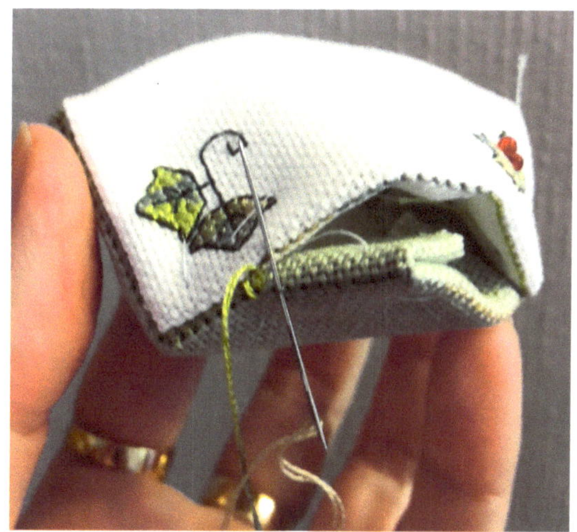

I hope you have found several biscornu pincushions you would like to stitch amongst the selection in the book. There are so many beautiful fabrics and threads that you have endless options.

But do be careful. It is difficult to stop after you have made three or four!

Happy stitching

Cherry

www.cherryparker.co.nz

NOTES

FURTHER BOOKS

FURTHER BOOKS

www.ingramcontent.com/pod-product-compliance
Lightning Source LLC
LaVergne TN
LVHW070216110826
845147LV00003B/590

* 9 7 8 0 4 7 3 7 7 8 6 7 5 *